Fortaleza

Fortaleza

Stories of Strength Drawn From Mind, Body, and Soul

Rocío Pérez and Co-Authors

Paperback ISBN: 9798873287468
Hardcover ISBN: 9798876516954

Edited by Roy Love and Shareen Rivera

Co-Authors: Adrianna Abarca, José Beteta, Tamil Maldonado Vega, Jerry Natividad, Gil Juarez, Martha Niño Rodriguez, Silvia Eliat, Carlos Quezada, Mark Madrid, Staci LaToison, Gerardo Garcia-Jurado, Pedro David Espinoza, Marcia V. Moreno, Saul Gomez, Joanne Siracusa, Pam Covarrubias, Mavi Barraza, Veronica Lawrence Ortega, Angélica Killion, Alejandra "Ale" Spray, Eduardo Villavicencio-Vizcaino

DEDICATION

To the readers of *Fortaleza*,

This dedication is a tribute to your strength and resilience. As you embark on this transformative journey, remember that you are not alone. The stories within these pages will inspire and empower you to overcome challenges and discover a world of possibilities.

Fortaleza is the strength of mind, body, and soul that helps navigate life's storms with grace. It fuels your dreams, turns obstacles into steppingstones, and teaches you valuable lessons. The co-authors, who have each faced challenges, share their experiences to inspire and educate others.

Embrace the power within to create your version of a happy, healthy, and meaningful life. Shift your perspective from "what's happening to me" *to* "what's happening *for* me." Realize that every challenge is an opportunity in disguise.

May *Fortaleza* guide you toward a life filled with resilience, growth, and endless potential.

Con Mucho Amor,

Co-Authors, *Fortaleza*

JEFFREY A. MARQUEZ

Colonel, U.S. Army (Retired) | Principal | Marquez Leadership,
Culture & Strategy, LLC

Jeff Marquez, founder of Marquez Leadership, Culture & Strategy, LLC, works with business, government, and nonprofit leaders who want to lead as their better self, build a winning team, and succeed sustainably. A retired Army officer and former senior executive with the federal government, Marquez served on the National Security Council as the Director of Continuity Policy and Acting Senior Director for Response Policy. He led the team that developed the successful US drawdown from Iraq in 2011. In Hawaii, he led the transformation of United States Army forces in the Pacific. He also served as a chief of staff in the federal government. He has led continuity and infectious disease planning actions across two administrations.

FOREWORD

Written by Jeffrey A. Marquez

Starting my own business in 2019 was a trepid proposition. I knew what I knew. I had 30-plus years of leading others in often high-pressure situations. I thought I could now share my experiences to help others achieve success. It seemed straightforward and doable. Yet, there were many unknowns that I didn't know. I didn't appreciate the time and effort that goes into creating content, programs, and my style. I also didn't appreciate the identity crux I was mired in after a career that valued my leadership while I contended with the longings for my cultura. In retrospect, I was responsible for my choices. I could have easily celebrated my Latinidad while serving, just as I did and still do while celebrating my Americanness. They are not mutually exclusive, and my identity journey is proving as much.

The stories you are about to experience with *Fortaleza* reveal how Latinidad and America are mutually supporting. Latinidad and America need each other. We know the stories of immigrants coming to America to make a better life for themselves and their families. As you experience *Fortaleza*, you will realize how these amazing people are making a better life for all Americans. There are also stories of second, third, and fourth-generation Americans who struggle with assimilation, identity, language, racism, colorism, and the yearning to hold onto their Latinidad. Not all may agree with their choices, though no one can deny their fortitude. You will realize how their stories are American stories. You will experience the challenges many of these leaders faced as they left everything they held dear, hoping for a greater way of life. You will experience pain and sorrow with them and the joy and happiness of winning, yes, winning because of their resilience, grit, determination, and their ability to turn pain and sorrow into success.

You are about to embark upon a uniquely American journey. From boardrooms to corporate suites, government and uniformed services to small businesses and startups, allow these stories to harness the collective power of our community, of our nation. Their content, programs, and styles emanate from their journeys, and their examples will be guideposts for years. And as our stories, differences, agreements — and disagreements — and our failures followed by triumphs become part of the unvarnished, transparent American story, our nation will be better and stronger.

With Gratitude,

Jeffrey A. Marquez
Colonel, U.S. Army (Retired)
Principal
Marquez Leadership, Culture & Strategy, LLC

Nancy Rosado-Santiago

TIME101 | HLX+

Nancy Rosado-Santiago is recognized as one of TIME101's most influential people. She currently holds the position of Chief Community & Media Officer at Amrak Solutions where she works with a team dedicated to creating purpose and innovation-driven platforms powered by digital media. A Corporate Social Responsibility award-winning program she leads is Capitanes del Futuro for Procter & Gamble and Major League Soccer, focusing on empowering Latino youth across the country. She leads a national non-profit collaborating with volunteers from the professional and corporate sectors bringing about sustainable change in underserved and underrepresented communities, particularly for the progress of youth. She is an award-winning advertising and media executive, having worked with major organizations throughout her career. Her expertise and leadership have been also notably recognized by national and local organizations such as the YMCA and New York City Hispanic Chamber of Commerce establishing her as a prominent figure in the Hispanic/Latinx realm in both community and corporate leadership.

FOREWORD

Written by Nancy Rosado-Santiago

Eighty-three percent of Latinos view the U.S. as a country of opportunity and 79% of Latinos say the U.S. is a country where they can get ahead in life.

"Fortaleza: Stories of Strength Drawn from Mind, Body, and Soul" is a beacon of hope, a collection of extraordinary real-life stories that illuminate the path to triumph.

Within the pages of this anthology, you will encounter a tapestry of diverse stories from individuals who have faced life's trials head-on. Their journeys, though unique, are bound together by a common thread of persistence, resilience, determination, and fortitude. These are stories of triumph over adversity in the face of unimaginable obstacles and of the unwavering belief in the power of the human spirit.

The co-authors of *"Fortaleza"* bring their varied backgrounds and experiences, weaving together a narrative that celebrates the beauty of diversity and the inherent strength that lives within each of us. Their stories serve as a reminder that strength is not limited to the physical form and encompasses the mind and soul as well. They invite us to embark on a journey of self-discovery and growth, to uncover the depths of our own fortitude.

As you turn the pages of *"Fortaleza,"* prepare to be moved and inspired, and even brought to tears. Each story is a testament to the resilience of the human spirit, calling on us to reflect upon the light that will shine even in the darkness. These stories will challenge you to confront your own obstacles, embrace your own *Fortaleza*, and believe in the limitless possibilities that live within you.

The creation of this book is a testament to the power of collaboration and the support of a remarkable network of friends, family, and colleagues. It is through their unwavering belief in the importance of sharing these stories that "*Fortaleza*" has come to life. The path towards its completion has widened the lens of perception, empathy, and human dignity, as the co-authors take a deep dive into their experiences, uncovering the strength that has propelled them forward.

I invite you to join us on this journey of strength and self-discovery. Let these stories ignite the fire within you, and may you find the courage to bring forth the very best of you to face the challenges that come your way, growing stronger and wiser with every challenge.

Together, let us celebrate the magnificence of the human spirit, for it is in our *Fortaleza* that we can find, nurture, and share our truest selves.

Mil Gracias,

Nancy Rosado-Santiago, *Lead with Love*
TIME101 | HLX+

MESSAGE FROM THE AUTHORS

What's the purpose of having wisdom if you do not share it? What's the point of overcoming adversity if you do not stop to open doors for others who are in the same situations you were once in? In this book, we, a group of Latino co-authors, have come together to share our collective wisdom and experiences. We aim to educate others about the struggles that Latinos experience in the United States, in the hopes that our culture can be better understood and embraced for the richness that it truly is, and to let other Latinos know that they are not alone.

We firmly believe in the importance of helping and giving back to others. By repurposing our pain, history, and experiences, we can uplift and support those around us, creating a better world for all. Throughout our individual journeys, we have faced numerous challenges and obstacles that have shaped us into the resilient individuals we are today. We have experienced the pain of leaving our homes, the heartbreak of separation from loved ones, and the adversity of navigating a new culture and language. However, instead of allowing these experiences to define us negatively, we have chosen to repurpose them for the greater good.

One of the key messages we want to convey is the power of empathy and compassion. By understanding and acknowledging our own struggles, we become more attuned to the experiences of others. This awareness enables us to extend a helping hand and provide support to those who need it most. Through volunteering, mentoring, and sharing our stories, we have witnessed firsthand the transformative impact of reaching out to others.

Furthermore, we emphasize the significance of repurposing our history. Our personal histories are filled with lessons and insights that can be invaluable to others. By sharing our stories, we not only inspire and empower those who may be going through similar experiences, but we also contribute to the collective wisdom of humanity. Our history becomes a tapestry of resilience, strength, and growth, reminding us that we are not alone in our struggles.

Lastly, we highlight the importance of repurposing our experiences. Every experience we go through, whether positive or negative, has the potential to shape us and teach us valuable lessons. By reflecting on these experiences and extracting wisdom from them, we can use our newfound knowledge to guide and support others. Our experiences become a wellspring of wisdom, offering guidance and inspiration to those who may be navigating similar paths.

As co-authors, we have come together with a shared vision of creating a book that not only celebrates the power of helping and giving back but also serves as a call to action for readers. We invite you to join us on this journey of self-discovery, empathy, and transformation. Together, let us repurpose our pain, history, and experiences to create a world where compassion and support are the guiding principles. Together, as we educate others about the struggles Latinos face, we can create a ripple effect of understanding, acceptance, and appreciation for the richness of our culture.

Table of Contents

INTRODUCTION

Fortaleza is a book about the strength of mind, body, and soul. Readers will be moved, inspired, motivated, and encouraged by the stories contained herein to see beyond their challenges, draw strength from them in the face of adversity, and realize a world never experienced before, a different world, because they, themselves, will be different.

In a world that often tests our limits, *Fortaleza* is the armor we need to face adversity head-on and emerge stronger. The unwavering strength within refuses to yield to life's challenges. It's the force that can turn the tide of any situation in our favor.

Experience a sense of connectedness with the co-authors' experiences and find the power from within to bring your own dreams to fruition as you create your own happy, healthy, meaningful life.

Fortaleza will help readers shift the narrative of "what's happening to me" to "what's happening for me" and realize that the magic we all look for is in the work that we often avoid. We already possess what we need to succeed: our wisdom, our energy, and our essence.

Fortaleza is the internal strength that helps navigate the storms of life with grace and determination. It is your most potent ally – it fuels your dreams, propels you forward, and turns obstacles into stepping stones to push through, learn, and grow and when you choose to embrace it wholeheartedly, you'll find that every challenge is an opportunity in disguise.

The twenty-two co-authors in this book are opening their lives and sharing their experiences to inspire and educate others. Many of them have faced complex challenges throughout their lives and believe that sharing their stories can help others avoid making the same mistakes or provide inspiration for those who may be going through similar struggles.

AUTHOR

ROCÍO PÉREZ

Creator | Author | Speaker | Trainer
The MindShift Game

Rocío Pérez is the Creator of *The MindShift Game®*, host of *The MindShift Game TV®*, and host of *Rompiendo Barreras con Rocío Pérez* podcast. She helps individuals take more courageous, consistent actions, build their confidence, tap into their power, and elevate their energy. She has successfully implemented personalized self-improvement programs on a global scale. Additionally, she's authored two books, *Unstoppable* and *Fortaleza*, and has contributed to various publications such as Hispanics Star, Latinas 100, and even the esteemed International Social Sciences Journal. A dynamic bilingual, bicultural leader, Rocío has nearly three decades of helping others to live a fulfilled life.

To learn more, visit www.TheMindShiftGame.com

I Once Was, Now I Am, and I Will Be ...

In every family, one person carries the torch of light and paves the way to freedom, healing, abundance, and love. This responsibility can be a lonely journey, filled with misunderstandings; we learn to live life alone, with a laser focus on living a better life. Once we reach the state of "light," we realize that tangible success is only a partial victory. The actual work lies in healing ourselves. Healing is an ongoing voyage of self-exploration, with countless layers and doors that lead to unexplored realms within us. The journey is a transformative process that extends beyond individual success, emphasizing the ongoing exploration of the intricate layers and uncharted territories within us, delving into the depths of the *mind, body, and soul.*

The Allegory of the Caves, written by Plato, describes prisoners living in a dark cave, trapped inside by the illusion of monstrous shadows on the wall. One prisoner broke free, discovering the beauty of the outside world – he went back to save the others, yet most chose to stay in the darkness out of fear of what was outside the cave. The escaped prisoner never returned to the cave after experiencing the warmth of the light and the tapestry of the world. The cave of ignorance is a prison that holds many captives their entire lives. Once we realize that we are the creators of our own lives, there is no going back to the dark cave.

We are all a product of our life experiences. For us to live a better life, we must *shift* our consciousness. In toxic environments, individuals often misconstrue what is right and wrong, perpetuating a cycle that persists due to familiarity. Sharing my truth is my way of furthering my healing and helping others heal and live a better life.

My Beginning

I am the daughter of Mexican parents and the only female and middle child of five children. I was born in Laredo, Texas – a small town known as the Devil's Belly Button, and I couldn't agree more as a better way to describe it.

My mom was raised in a traditional *machista* (chauvinistic) family in the border towns of Laredo, Texas, and Nuevo Laredo, Mexico. Her dream was to marry and have a career as an accountant. My father was a free-spirited Mexican immigrant who left home at 17 to explore the U.S. My parents met, fell in love, and quickly married. On their wedding night, my father took my mother's clothes, makeup, and everything he fell in love with, and threw it all in the trash, saying, "That *was* your life." My father was resourceful, hard-working, and charismatic, and provided for his family most of the time. He was controlling, limiting our interactions with the outside world. My mother became a stay-at-home mom and hated her life.

My father's impulsive behavior caused frequent relocations during my childhood; his drinking or fighting often got him fired. His sudden job losses meant we had little time to pack, sometimes only hours. If we were lucky, we'd grab a grocery bag full of clothes on our way out the door. My mom was used to his chaotic behavior and kept certain items ready to go. She grabbed her portable one-burner tabletop stove, rolling pin, a homemade *comal* (griddle), and a makeup caboodle filled with our family's important documents and photos.

Always lacking the necessities, my mom situated our family in each new city by registering us for school and applying for food stamps. Sometimes it took weeks to get benefits. My father hustled to put food on the table and a roof over our heads. When I was seven, I remember once we only had a gallon of milk and a loaf of bread for five children and two adults. We eagerly dipped our sliced bread into the milk, wanting to absorb as much goodness as possible, yet each bland, cold, wet mouthful left us yearning for more.

When others were around, my mom pretended we had a great life. She painted herself as a loving, caring, compassionate mother who wanted the best for her children, yet our reality was far from that. My mom did not want to be a mother and hated the responsibility of it. As her children, we kept her from living her dreams. *I got the worst of it.*

From my earliest memory, I suffered extreme physical, mental, and emotional abuse at the hands of my parents, as well as sexual abuse by my father. I slept on the cold cement floor, using a lace curtain as a blanket, and was woken up at 2 A.M. to cook my father's lunch before being allowed to go back to bed. I'd be woken up again at 5 A.M. to iron clothes, cook breakfast for the family, and get my younger brothers ready for school before I could get myself ready for the day.

I felt like an impostor within my family. I daydreamed of one day being rescued by my "real parents." My respite from my horrific homelife. was school. I escaped through my imagination and dreamt of being safe, loved, and cared for. I saw other girls living carefree and happy with their families, wearing beautiful clothes and backpacks full of school supplies. *I wanted to be them.*

I hung on to every thread of hope that my family would someday accept me, I was threatened to keep silent about my gruesome reality or risk harsher consequences. My uncles and aunts felt helpless as they witnessed my mom brutally beat me, yet they were unwilling to risk hurting her feelings and damaging their relationship – so they kept quiet. My mother not only withheld affection from me; she actively prevented others from forming connections with me or expressing kindness. Throughout the day, she belittled me and called me names that no other human being should be called.

During my childhood, I was stuck in the quicksand of destruction, which few people make it out of. By eleven, I recognized the pattern of poverty and abuse and the culture of silence that lay deep beneath the facade of normalcy. My family bonded over domestic violence, alcoholism, and crime and shut out anyone who questioned our distorted reality. Those who did were silenced and ostracized. The shame of my past muddied my worth. By twelve, I began smoking, drinking, and partying to numb the pain of the physical and psychological turmoil I had endured.

I had enough! I was no longer willing to be subjected to physical, sexual, and mental abuse.

At fourteen, I ran away with my twenty-two-year-old boyfriend. The trauma I experienced tainted the lens through which I saw him. Being a product of domestic violence, his violent, erratic behavior was normal and not nearly as bad as what I had experienced. At fifteen, I became a teen mom, and to government officials, I was seen as another statistic–a Mexican-American runaway girl. The birth of my son gave me strength to keep moving toward my dreams of becoming a teacher. He did not stand a chance in the world without a solid foundation for him to thrive. I vowed to give him that and more; I had to leave my comfort zone, make great sacrifices, and take extraordinary risks to create a better life for us.

That summer, with a sixth-grade education, I emancipated myself from my parents, enrolled in college, and embarked on the journey that led me here today. I cared for my family, commuted to and from school for up to four hours each way, and slept only three hours a night for years to reach my goals.

At nineteen, I was single and caring for my four-year-old son by myself, attending college, and working multiple jobs to build a future for us. My mother told me I would fail in college and that I should stay home, take care of a husband, and tend to my child instead. I lived the life my mother wished she would have lived, and she resented me for it. While she bragged about my accomplishments publicly, on the inside she wanted me to fail. My parents refused to attend any of my graduation ceremonies or events recognizing my achievements.

Regardless of my parents' lack of support, I was willing to make the necessary sacrifices to achieve my goals. This required me to step out of my comfort zone, do things that were foreign to me, and stop associating with loved ones so that I could reconcile my past, make new friends, and create a better life for us. I nurtured my son into the man I envisioned him to be, worked multiple jobs, and completed two associates, a bachelor's, a dual master's degree, and a graduate certification.

Throughout my life, I faced numerous challenges and adversities that could have easily defined me. Being a woman, Latina, a dropout, a teen mother, and the youngest in the group, societal expectations and judgments constantly surrounded me. However, I refused to let these circumstances limit my potential. Instead, I chose to define myself and pave my own path to success. I am the creator of my life, the author of my story, and the editor of my history. Despite my hardships, I have chosen to keep striving for success. My successes in life are a testament to my resilience, determination, and unwavering spirit. I'm proud of how far I've come and excited for the future I'm creating.

Through writing, I have discovered harmful family patterns and how my parents' experiences shaped their reality, subsequently affecting me. Abuse is never justified, however, by understanding my parents' stories, I've been able to forgive and embrace them with an open heart. My parents lacked the consciousness to do better and did not question their actions. I made a deliberate choice to study my life so I can break free from the destructive patterns engraved in my psyche. Love is what truly heals.

I spent most of my life in what I call "high-thriving survival mode," constantly striving to make something out of nothing while overcoming countless challenges. It took a brain tumor to wake me up and force me to acknowledge the painful past I had subconsciously compartmentalized so that I could live a somewhat normal life. It was like I had taken a black box filled with my traumatic life experiences, welded it shut, and dropped it in the middle of the ocean, never to be seen again.

My doctor said I could have a stroke and die at any moment. The news compelled me to reflect on what I wanted to do for the rest of my days. I had a desire to keep making a positive impact on people, and my love for coaching was already a part of my professional life. It required a life-threatening experience to awaken me to the fact that coaching wasn't just a passion; it was my calling and had the potential to become a viable business.

At 35, I delved deep into my journey of self-healing, trying to break free from the strictness that had defined my upbringing: the people-pleasing, perfectionist, and workaholic tendencies. I was like a fish out of water. For more than a decade I studied daily and learned from Oprah Winfrey, Alan Watts, Niurka, Claude Bristol, Anthony Robbins, Marianne Williamson, T. Harv Eker, Bob Proctor, and many others. I confirmed my natural competency in coaching and now had a name for the powerful techniques I had used for almost two decades. No one teaching had the magic formula to transform my life. I discovered we have the innate capacity to overcome challenges and create the life we love. I deciphered what worked for me and repeated it until I achieved my desired results – *The MindShift Game* was born from that experience. I created this process to help myself, used it with my clients, and gamified it so that people from all walks of life can achieve their desires.

Present: Where I Am Now

Sharing my complete story with raw vulnerability hasn't always been easy for me. Honestly, there are still moments when it's challenging. However, I understand that it's only through being fully vulnerable that I can truly support others on their own journeys. One of the ways I assist others in staying empowered and intentional in their own paths is by drawing from my own life experiences. I openly share my successes and failures to inspire and provide support. By reflecting on our own lives, we gain the ability to regulate our nervous system and make intentional choices instead of reacting impulsively. This self-reflection is crucial.

Every person has a unique journey with desires, goals, and aspirations and has the capacity to create a life they love and desire. I am reminded of a powerful quote by Dinos Christianopoulos, "They tried to bury us, and they did not know we were seeds." This quote resonates deeply with me because it speaks to the resilience and potential within each individual.

Moreover, I firmly believe in Alan Weiss's words, "Life is not a search for meaning; life is about the creation of meaning." Meaning and purpose are not something we find externally. We create them within ourselves, and our results are manifested in the material world.

I have acknowledged my abuse, danced with my pain, consoled my sorrows, and mined the gifts in my adversity. Through my journey, I learned that growth is constant. The most rewarding moments come from mastering my mind, and doing what it takes to transcend my life experiences and how I view the world. Every experience offers new knowledge and insights that shape my consciousness. I would not change anything about my life as it has shaped me into the conscious person that I am. I am continuously resolving my past to limit its negative impacts on my future.

Overcoming our fears, triggers, and roadblocks to success requires intentional effort and risk-taking. Pushing boundaries is a natural part of moving forward and truly living. Despite being advised against taking risks most of my life, I am proud of what I have accomplished because of it. If I were to do things differently, I might explore more resources and alternative ways of achieving my goals sooner, yet I would still choose to fail forward.

The person I have become through facing challenges has fostered compassion, empathy, connection, and community. It required asking myself about my greater purpose and fulfilling that purpose. Often, I have taken action even when it was difficult. In doing so, I discovered my true potential and made a meaningful impact on myself and others.

Beneath the challenges and obstacles, we face in our trauma, there is a lesson. That lesson, through the pain, is our hidden treasure. It's crucial to fully understand and learn from it so you can grow and avoid being in a vicious cycle. The question many ask is *How do I do this*. My 85-year-old mentor, Dr. Martha Urioste, once told me to tap into and channel my anger while using it as fuel to cut off negative influences and do better. While I didn't resonate with anger, I understood her point. Each person needs to find what motivates and fuels them to surpass their limitations and live life on their terms. For me, it was breaking free from my family, societal norms, and stereotypes. People trying to control me and dictate what I can or cannot do is what pushes me to prove that it is possible for me. When I'm told I can't do something, that often serves as fuel to propel me forward.

My mother's words haunted me in the past. She used to tell me I was worthless and would never amount to anything. Yet I used that as motivation to become more than she thought I could be. I understood that my brain was the most powerful tool because through it I can create my thoughts, feelings, beliefs, and actions to push myself to expand my capacity and strive for more. I took responsibility, re-parented myself, rewired my brain, and created a fruitful life for me and my son. In my career, I guide people to discover how they got to where they are today, what they are doing at this moment that is shaping their future, and what they intentionally choose to do to have what they want in their lives.

We must strongly desire a better life and be willing to do whatever it takes to transform ourselves into the people we aspire to be. Similar to how a personal trainer guides us toward the most effective exercises for us, we are the only ones who can put in the effort and do the necessary work to get what we desire. My coaching approach centers on affirmations, visualizations, bold actions, and beliefs. I believe in the power of a positive mindset and help individuals to instill empowering beliefs that support their goals.

My Life's Work

My upbringing and life experiences have led me to my mission: that every child lives a happy, healthy, and meaningful life. Children need to grow up in a loving and nurturing home where they are cherished, embraced, and supported so that they can become the best version of themselves and live a fulfilled life. The fable of the "Four Philanthropists" that Dr. Wayne Dyer used to share encapsulates the essence of my life's work:

"In a village, during a time of conquest, the men were taken and imprisoned in a war camp. Four village philanthropists assisted the men in various ways. One provided clean water, another offered bedding and blankets, and the third cultivated and supplied food. These philanthropists believed they had fulfilled their purpose by improving the living conditions of the prisoners.

Yet, the fourth philanthropist, a remarkably virtuous person, went beyond mere comfort and the limits of ordinary human awareness. This individual found the whereabouts of the prison keys and liberated the prisoners.

This tale teaches us that even though we can suffer in comfort there are people who can help set us free. By seeking out these individuals, we can transcend our limitations and find true liberation from our suffering."

I am the Fifth Philanthropist. I liberated myself, guided others to find their freedom, and then showed them how to free others from a place of love. We now can all be on a path of healing and freedom.

CULTURE, ARTS & ENTERTAINMENT

ADRIANNA ABARCA

Founder/ Board Chair,
The Latino Cultural Center in Denver, Colorado

Adrianna Abarca is the Founder/Board Chair of the Latino Cultural Arts Center, was a thirteen-year board member and co-founder of the Latino Community Foundation of Colorado and served five years on the board of the *Museo de las Américas*. For forty years, Abarca has worked to preserve and represent Latino cultural identities and to ensure a comprehensive and accurate representation of Latino contributions to history. Abarca hopes to leave a legacy of learning and cultural pride for generations of Latinos and strives to teach young people about the value of passion, hard work, and dedication.

Dream It, Believe It, Achieve It

I grew up in Denver, Colorado, the daughter of a determined Mexican immigrant dad and a hard-working Irish American mom who was orphaned at a young age. My father raised his three children greatly appreciating our Mexican heritage. He drove the family often to central Mexico to see family, and southern Mexico to explore. These trips helped me form a strong cultural identity. As a child, I searched high and low for library books containing insight into our Mexican-American and *Mexicano* history and culture to no avail. When my father returned from his travels to numerous Latin American countries, he brought home intriguing insights into beautiful cultures that I longed to find out more about, but those materials were also missing. This led me to wonder why this exclusion of knowledge.

I was fortunate that Denver was a stronghold for those demanding social change and civil rights starting in the 1970s and throughout my formative years. During the Chicano Movement, known as "*El Movimiento,*" there was a call for and a deep desire to educate ourselves about the lost histories and cultures of our people. As a community, we were deprived of that knowledge because it was ignored or taken from us by the school systems throughout the Southwest. As children, we weren't taught the histories and contributions of Latinos or any people of color in the United States, nor did we learn about Latin America. Today, we have access to many beautiful bilingual and bi-cultural books written for and by Latinos and important documentation online. If a child sees someone who looks like them and reads about similar experiences and accomplishments, it can instill pride, satisfaction, and a sense of hope. You will always feel like an "outsider" if you're not exposed to others like you who have found success. If adults are proud and knowledgeable about their culture and history, they can have the satisfaction of sharing their learnings and sense of belonging with others, especially children.

I was raised primarily with kids whose families had deep roots in Southern Colorado and Northern New Mexico. Most had no ties to or understanding of their ancestral cultures. The majority of us didn't speak Spanish, let alone have a solid historical understanding of our families' contributions to the development of what is today the Southwest U.S. We all struggled with "belonging" because it was not possible to relate to our parents' experiences of discrimination since the hatred had become less blatant, and our parents did their best to shield us from it. We felt pressured to turn our backs on the Spanish language. This loss was an essential part of the uncomfortable cultural norms that were imposed by a society that was determined to assimilate us. My peers and I felt "out of place" and not valued, but we could not express or understand why we didn't fit into the mold society was trying to squeeze us into.

Not speaking, reading, and writing in Spanish well is highly disadvantageous. It significantly limits one's ability to communicate with many nearby people and a big part of Latin America. We were often told while growing up that English was the only language we needed. Nothing could be further from the truth. Ignoring a link as valuable as the language of one's culture is a tremendous loss, and the fastest way society was able to cut a valuable link to our heritage. Today many Native cultures are working hard to revive their original ancestral language. No one should be limited to just one language. Other worlds open to you with every new language you learn. Fully understanding other ways to communicate is beautiful and enhances life on many levels. Most of my peers didn't learn Spanish, which oftentimes led to frustration and embarrassment. They felt ashamed for not being able to speak it, and fluent Spanish speakers couldn't comprehend why so many who had Spanish surnames and whose parents spoke Spanish didn't. This lack of ability to communicate easily led to unnecessary tension and conflict between Mexican Americans and *Mexicanos* that exist to this day.

I had to work very hard to "recuperate" my Spanish. In retrospect, many things kept me from learning Spanish well. Although my father was fluent, my mother was not, so they defaulted to English at home. In addition to our parents not speaking Spanish to us, Denver schools didn't introduce Spanish until Junior High and society did not encourage speaking Spanish in public. It was difficult traveling to Mexico and not being able to communicate freely with family. Regretfully, I shunned Spanish until I went to college and came to realize I had been deprived of an essential cultural component and valuable skill. I regret the missed opportunities and awkward interactions that I endured for so many years.

I attended Denver North High School, where I met one of my first mentors, Vice Principal Dr. Martha Urioste, who strongly encouraged me to attend university. Very few Mexican American girls were encouraged to enter higher education back then. The fact that my older brother went to college helped me to see that I could also do it, but I would have to figure out how to apply independently. Dr. Urioste was the only person to push me to study beyond high school, and she wrote numerous letters of recommendation, which I found very encouraging. I also credit *El Movimiento* for my access to a college degree and the opportunity to take Chicano and Latin American History and Literature classes at the university. After taking many invaluable courses, I was able to pinpoint some of what led to the confusion and angst I experienced growing up. Today, I dedicate myself to helping others learn more about and embrace their culture. That knowledge enables them to share what makes them unique with others, while at the same time finding commonalities.

Little did I know the culture shock that attending Denver University, a small private school, would be for my first year of college. I didn't feel like I belonged there, even though it was in my own "backyard." For the first time in my life, I was surrounded by students who had grown up entitled in prosperous communities with access to better education. I was not socially or academically well prepared and went home practically every weekend. For my second year, I transferred to the University of Colorado in Boulder (CU), hoping to find more diversity. There were still many challenges, some of them academic, but I found my community when I joined the UMAS (United Mexican American Students) and MeCHA (*Movimiento Estudiantil Chicano de Aztlán*) clubs. These groups didn't exist at my previous school. I needed to find peers, though few, who had experienced many of the same difficulties I had growing up and knew how it felt to attend a college with a limited racial makeup.

We need mentors to succeed. One of my most significant college courses was an Introduction to Chicano Literature class with Dr. Cordelia Candelaria. Soon after, she invited me to do my work study in the Chicano Studies Department. Having the Latin American Studies program and Dr. Candelaria's support helped me stay engaged. For my third year of college, I had the opportunity to study abroad in Spain where I immersed myself in Spanish culture, which ironically also contributed to my struggle with cultural identity. I didn't feel a genuine connection to the Spaniards, despite many similarities, because of my unique cultural experiences from having grown up in the Southwest. I also felt some anger towards them, knowing that their ancestors were so brutal to the Natives of the Americas. Focusing on Latin American Studies at CU allowed me to appreciate the fantastic variances of Latinos in the Americas and the strength in that diversity.

Being a multi-racial and multi-ethnic person has been a blessing. It's an incredible advantage to relate to multiple ethnicities and cultures. If you visit countries where people are varied, for example, Colombia or Venezuela, it's acknowledged that most of their people are of mixed race. Diverse communities understand that we're all in the "same boat" and can only succeed if we work together. As *Latino Americanos* we are more likely to be of mixed race, have common ancestry, and are likely to share a similar history. In this New World, most of us, native and immigrant alike, are descendants of conquered or subjugated people. Regardless of this understanding, sadly, discrimination still exists based on race, skin color, religion, and ethnicity. Our diversity is invaluable and gives us different sources of strength to pull from for inspiration, motivation, and pride.

Those of us of Mexican heritage are very fortunate for our proximity to Mexico. It is much harder for other Latinos from further away to find themselves and thrive in North America. Living in the Southwest U.S., it is common and easy for families to travel to Mexico. If you hail from Southern Mexico, Central America, the Caribbean, and South America, it is difficult to reconnect to the homeland; It's more challenging to hold on to the connection with family and cultural traditions. As Mexicans, we must acknowledge and be grateful for all the benefits our proximity to our homeland brings. I have heard it said that Latin America is where Latinos are. It's amazing how many Latin Americans have recently immigrated to Spain. Will their children have a connection to their parents' traditions through family or new communities, and will Spaniards be more willing to share the accurate history and the varied cultures of the new arrivals with their children in schools? As descendants of Spaniards, many Latinos have lost that connection to Spain here in the Americas, but will that also change? Now that many *Latino Americanos* are living a "reverse migration," will Spain become an extension of Latin America in the way that Latin America is seen as an extension of Spain?

I often consider how one "type" of Latino relates to another in a social setting. What makes us unique, and what do we have in common? Should unity among Latinos be encouraged, forsaking what makes us different, or should we maintain and promote a greater understanding and tolerance of our inherent diversity? The term *Latinidad* is not all-inclusive, nor is it just one thing. For me, *Latinidad* is a feeling of unity among Latinos. It refers to shared cultural commonalities and similarities, for example, in our food, music, and customs. This term acknowledges our diversity and unique sense of pride, while simultaneously being part of something bigger than oneself. It is so much more inclusive than being labeled "Hispanic" or *Hispano*, because of a person's surname. For people of mixed heritage, like Native, African, and Asian, this title over-emphasizes Spanish blood, even though many Latinos have little or no Spanish ancestry. Many Latinos are mixed race, and most haven't had a direct connection to Spain for centuries, whereas others are of other European descent.

A good education is indispensable. Women need to go on to higher education, and Latino parents need to encourage them. It's hard for young women in our communities to leave home to study elsewhere. Culturally, we impose many unjustifiable fears on young girls about going too far from the protection of family. Historically, young Latinas were expected to marry at an early age, although the norms are starting to change. For young girls, it is crucial for the family to create an expectation early on so that there's an assumption that young ladies will continue on to higher education, vocational school, or some other form of professional training. We must nurture an insatiable appetite for learning so that when the system fails to provide a good education, an individual is resilient enough to find a path around it. Additionally, having an international experience helped me see the world differently, and I am a better person because of it. I always encourage young people to seek out travel as a valuable part of their education. It is essential to help our children better understand the world we live in. This will help them be more attuned to the benefits of living in a diverse world that embraces differences rather than fighting them.

Sometimes, we cling to tradition because we can't see the benefits of change. Generations ago, there was an economic necessity to keep the family close. If someone went off to college, they would not contribute to the household income, which is still very real for many families. I noticed in the Chicano community that there was a fear that someone could go further than you because they were better educated and knew things you didn't know. This fear created insecurity and feelings of inferiority. Individuals may know about or have access to something they did not, which makes them apprehensive. There is tremendous pressure to be like everyone else, to conform, assimilate, and not stand out as an individual. For example, kids in school are pressured to dress like everyone else, watch sports, make English their primary or sole language, and acculturate. Some of this is changing, thanks to globalization, the internet, and more accessible access to information. There are still many things that we are pressured to conform to, certain norms considered part of "being American."

The value of traditions is that they can be the "glue" that holds a community together. We must let our youth recognize and remember where their family members came from and the experiences they had. One way to help children understand their culture and identity is to have them read about it through children's books. You must nurture an insatiable appetite for learning, starting with good reading habits at a young age. If an individual does not have access to a good education through the system, they must have the means to get around it, either by accessing books or the internet or gaining knowledge directly as an apprentice.

I am dedicated to telling our stories, sharing our cultural expressions, and ensuring that all Latinos are well-represented in the U.S.

and elsewhere. We must have the most accurate representation possible to improve this world. It is on each of us to work to make sure that our stories are told accurately and completely. We have many successful and accomplished people from the past and present, and we need to hear more about them. Cultural identity, usually learned by family and one's proximate community, is key to a person's well-being and sense of belonging. If cultural heritage is not solidified by family traditions or offered in the educational systems, individuals will look for outside groups and experiences to feel included and bring definition to their lives. Exclusion is almost always deliberate, and a blunt tool to inflict doubt and harm. I believe many established institutions are intentionally exclusionary, even if some of the staff are unaware of this deliberate approach to weeding out.

The creation of the Latino Cultural Arts Center (LCAC) in Denver was born out of my frustration with the existing institutions and their inadequacies in representing and supporting the cultural growth of the Latino youth in Denver and the Southwest. Our arts organizations are few, usually poorly funded, and don't serve enough people. Founders generally come to the table with little or no experience and do the very best possible job without sufficient support. Working with existing well-funded mainstream museums showed me how few of our people are sufficiently educated to work in the more important positions and are rarely given an opportunity to apprentice. Few Latinos are present in the administration and curation of museum and gallery exhibits, and when culturally relevant shows are presented, most often they fall short in content. My goal is to provide unique points of entry into the arts for educators, families, and youth, and to create occasions that encourage people to travel and share or develop their skills.

Part of my dream is to lead the creation of an entire Latino cultural campus in central Denver, where the history and artistic expressions of Latino communities are represented region-wide.

I'm committed to creating meaningful places for scholars, families, and artists to unite and serve diverse Latino communities and celebrate the work and heritage of Latino creators from far-reaching locations. My team and I are in the process of opening a community visual and media arts space entitled *Las Bodegas* in 2024. We will offer creative guidance and technical instruction in English and Spanish to people of varying ages and skill levels. Additionally, part of the vision for the LCAC is to create a Mexican Heritage Museum, or *Museo de Herencia Mexicana*, which will house the Abarca Family Collection of Chicano and *Mexicano* folk & fine art and a Latin American research library.

My advice to Latinas and Latinos striving to succeed in this world is simple: What you're trying to accomplish may scare you or seem unattainable. Have a conversation with yourself every day and reaffirm your abilities and dedication. Tell yourself that you're going to figure it out. There will be days when you're the only person who understands what you are trying to achieve; don't let this scare you. Success can be lonely, so you must be very self-assured. Silence your doubt with, "I'm going to figure this out. I'm going to do this." Be your greatest advocate and admirer. As women, we must take or make opportunities, push open doors, and hold them open for others. Latinos must be decisive about demonstrating our abilities and creating our own models of success. If you're not curious or don't want to learn more about what you're taking on, you need to find something else to give your energy to. Keep looking until you find something you experience and dream about every day; find your passion.

JOSÉ BETETA

Co-Founder/CEO,

Raíces Brewing Company

Born in Costa Rica as the second oldest of 8 siblings, José was the first one in his family to attend and finish College, earning a Business and IT degree from Howard University. He came to the U.S. as a child and spent 28 years undocumented, navigating complexities and challenges. Nevertheless, José persevered, becoming a vocal public figure for immigrant and human rights, an advocate for small and minority businesses, and a supporter of entrepreneurship.

Currently, José and his COO wife partner at Raíces Brewing Company, where he, as CEO oversees all areas of this wildly successful enterprise.

LIKE A RIVER

What really is resilience? When people talk about resilience, it is often implied as if a person simply endures and survives, like a strong oak weathering a storm. I believe that resilience is a crucial factor in achieving success, but I've come to understand that it is so much more than only enduring. Resilience has more to do with applying yourself strategically because survival in this world is not always as straightforward as being the strongest or fittest. It requires a combination of strength and adaptability, using your brain to navigate and adapt to different situations.

In my own experience, I have found that imagining myself as a river has helped me survive and thrive. Like a river, I flow and find alternative paths when faced with obstacles. If I encounter a brick wall or a rock, I try to go around it, always seeking the ocean. I have learned that a straight line is not always the most effective path to achieving my goals. Instead, I adapt to new realities and situations, constantly evolving as a person. When a river encounters obstacles like dams or walls, its energy accumulates and becomes even stronger. Similarly, in life, when we face challenges and barriers, we have the opportunity to strengthen our core values and build a solid foundation. Community has always been a fundamental value for me, and it is through the support and connections within my community that I have found strength and resilience.

As a first-generation immigrant to this country, the support of others has played a crucial role in doors being opened for me that I couldn't necessarily open myself no matter how hard I worked. I was able to gain people's support by fostering relationships with people in my community. It's not about what you can get from people, but what you can give. Building strong relationships is also crucial in navigating through life. Being able to connect with different communities, people, and cultures is a valuable asset. By creating relationships with diverse groups, we gain a broader perspective and open ourselves up to new opportunities and experiences.

Like many other Latin American countries during that time, Costa Rica also faced financial difficulties in the early 90's. While it may be perceived as a paradise by some, it is important to acknowledge that it is not the case for everyone. My parents decided to move from here and embarked towards the U.S. promised land. After trekking a journey with four small children, crossing multiple Central American countries in turmoil, spending time in jails in Mexico and California, Coyotes, Witches, and other things frankly meriting their own book, we made it to the U.S. My parents had to work two to three jobs each to make ends meet for our family of four to survive. Our lives were filled with constant activity, attending school, and participating in extracurricular activities to stay occupied. From a young age, I drew inspiration from my parents' relentless work ethic, especially after we came to the United States when I was twelve-years old. Witnessing their dedication and sacrifice motivated me to push myself and strive for success. I felt a sense of responsibility to make the most out of the opportunities they were providing for me. No one had to explicitly tell me to work hard, it was ingrained in me by observing their tireless efforts.

Their example taught me the value of perseverance and instilled in me a drive to achieve something meaningful in my life. I understood that their sacrifices were made with the hope that I would have a better future. This realization fueled my determination to make the most out of the opportunities presented to me and to create a successful path for myself. By my second year, I had achieved fluency in English. In high school, I excelled in English proficiency and ranked in the top five percent of my class. I was even a member of the National Honor Society. I was the only one in my family to attend college, and I eventually inspired my younger sibling to do the same. I was fortunate to receive a soccer scholarship and later a science scholarship to Howard University, where I earned a Bachelor's Degree in Information Systems and Business Administration. My drive to succeed was also influenced by my citizenship status. When I immigrated to the U.S. from Costa Rica at the age of twelve, my family and I were undocumented. While my family was able to resolve their immigration status within eight years, I faced numerous obstacles. Unfortunately, due to a dishonest attorney who attempted to exploit my family for more money, I aged out of the process and remained in a state of legal limbo. I was now too old to take advantage of the help my family was able to benefit from, and if I tried to state my case in court for some kind of clemency, the stakes were too high for deportations, no matter how good of a case I may have had. The legal climate at that moment in the White House and Congress was all about leveraging immigration levels for political points. This is when I learned how politics use immigrants as pawns. It wasn't until 2019 that I finally obtained my residency. For nearly twenty-eight years, I lived without legal status, but I remained resilient and determined. I became the first in my family to attend college, driven by a desire to achieve as much as possible despite my circumstances. I wanted to be in a strong position in case any legal challenges arose, and I wanted to prove myself as a valuable member of the community. I strived to be an exemplary individual, ready to present my case to a judge if necessary, highlighting my educational achievements and contributions to society.

When I was at Howard University, I had the opportunity to work for a chemistry professor in their environmental and atmospheric science program. This job allowed me to work closely with NASA, as I was involved in their grants and other projects. It was an incredible experience, especially because I was working alongside my professor in the atmospheric science program. One day, my professor approached me and asked if I wanted to join a trip. Due to a conflict, one of their graduate students couldn't make it, and they needed someone to help with atmospheric measurements. The purpose of the trip was to study the impact of particles from storms originating in Western Africa and traveling to the Caribbean. I was excited about the opportunity, but I hadn't mentioned to my professor that I didn't have citizenship.

Eventually, I gathered the courage to tell my professor about my situation. I was worried about being kicked out of school and not being able to re-enter the country if I went on the trip. However, my professor was incredibly understanding and supportive. They assured me that it wouldn't be a problem. At the time, I had a driver's license, which was sufficient for traveling to Puerto Rico. So, I decided to go on the trip. I flew to Puerto Rico and waited for the ship to arrive. From there, we embarked on a seven-day journey to New Orleans. It was an amazing experience and being in Puerto Rico felt like being close to my home country, Costa Rica.

Although my mom was initially concerned about me not being able to return to the country, I convinced her that this was a once-in-a-lifetime opportunity. I felt a strong urge to take this trip, and I couldn't ignore it. Thankfully, everything turned out well. During the trip, I had the chance to meet a Puerto Rican professor from another university who was also participating in the study. We instantly connected but didn't continue to talk after the trip because we were both in a relationship at the time. A year later, while walking through my university's campus, I unexpectedly ran into her. We reconnected, and eventually, the Puerto Rican professor, Tamil Maldonado, became my wife. It was through this experience that I learned the importance of listening to our intuition, and taking risks that it urges us to take even when we won't have the understanding or support from others. For first-generation immigrants to this country, that can be a difficult thing, especially for those who don't have their citizenship because there is a lot of fear in our space of being caught so we settle for living life on eggshells. However, I share this story to encourage you to not lose that part of yourself that seeks more and is willing to risk it all for a chance for that more. That part of us is often the part that will take us to the next level.

My wife has by far been my biggest supporter, ally, and best friend. Having that one person in your corner makes all the difference in the world. I know it did for me, especially during one of the most difficult periods of my life. When I reached the age of thirty, I found myself in a challenging situation where I couldn't secure employment due to my citizenship status. I relied on side gigs and contract work as a web designer to generate income, but it wasn't enough. My wife became the sole provider for our household during this time, and it was a difficult period for me. I was stuck in a mindset that limited my options and prevented me from exploring other ways to make money. However, through conversations with my wife, I was able to break free from that mindset. I realized that there are multiple paths to success, just like many rivers leading to the same ocean. I had been so focused on one approach that I had overlooked other opportunities available to me. Although this period of my life was very difficult for me, I appreciate the strength that my marriage gained as a result of it. As you face challenges together, you start to truly appreciate the value of the person by your side. You begin to recognize the strength and support your partner provides, and it becomes a significant aspect of your relationship. As you navigate through life, you uncover new layers and discover even more wonderful qualities in your partner and recognize how you don't even deserve this person right now but they're still here by your side, supporting and loving you. It really is the challenges you overcome together that only strengthen the bond you share. When facing challenges, it's important to remember how you overcame them and the people who supported you along the way. Many people believe they navigate life alone, like a grain of salt or a drop of water. However, the small contributions others make to your life are incredibly valuable. These little golden nuggets add up to create a beautiful life. Unfortunately, sometimes we realize the importance of expressing gratitude when those people are no longer present.

In 2016, I started working for The Chamber of Commerce, and during this time The Chamber of Commerce was in a state of disarray, it was almost non-existent. I initially thought I would just be a member, but then the previous president surprised me by saying, "Congratulations, you're the new president." I was taken aback and had to quickly figure out how to navigate the role. It was a daunting task. However, during my time at the chamber, I formed valuable relationships and learned a great deal. I gained knowledge about business plans, connected with local, state, and national officials, and became well-versed in legislation and available resources. These experiences allowed me to not only benefit myself but also pass on valuable information to other businesses and entrepreneurs. The chamber has now transformed into a hub for Latinos, providing resources and information to other businesses and entrepreneurs in need. We have become a trusted source for agencies like small business development centers, who seek to share important information with minorities and Latinos. During my time at the Chamber of Commerce, I had the opportunity to assist numerous small businesses within the community. Through this experience, I came to understand that one of the most significant mistakes an individual can make in business is failing to educate themselves adequately and not seeking assistance when needed. It is common for people to face challenges alone, keeping their struggles hidden due to fear and shame. However, it is important to recognize that there are resources within communities that can provide support to small businesses. To access these resources, one must be willing to step outside their comfort zone and ask for help.

Working within a community has always been a strong support for me and my wife. I have encountered many situations where communities prefer to work in isolation, but I have always believed that this is a mistake. When communities come together and collaborate, the results can be truly remarkable. I have witnessed firsthand how opening up and working together can benefit everyone involved, especially the community itself. In March 2014, Boulder City Council appointed me as the first undocumented commissioner in the country. I accepted this unanimous appointment to represent my community in the Human Relations Commission, to uphold human rights, to advise the City Council, and to make decisions in this quasi-judicial position. This was a risky, yet bold move by my community to invest in me despite my status, by focusing on my strengths, values, and my views on investing back in people. I will always value this moment because it allowed me to come out of the fear and shadows of my status to become a more productive member of society henceforth.

Community and family are core values for me and my wife, and with that idea in mind, my wife and I started a cultural program called Barrio E' Centro, which was a multicultural center aimed at celebrating Latino culture in all its diversity. We rented a space in Longmont, Colorado, with the initial intention of organizing programs for the community to enjoy. However, it quickly became apparent that the community wanted to use the space to host their own programs. About ninety percent of the programs ended up being organized by the community themselves, which was amazing to see. Unfortunately, we had to close down when the building we rented was sold for a couple million dollars. An amount that we couldn't afford. Instead of immediately finding another place, we took some time to rethink our goals. At the time, I was attending a leadership program at the Latino Leadership Institute in Colorado, and during a brainstorming session, the idea of a Latino brewery came up. I had mentioned it casually during a conversation with friends after the session, and it seemed like a great idea. So, during the next brainstorming session, I brought up the idea and received positive feedback. I realized that there were very few Latino breweries compared to the total number of breweries in the country, making it a viable concept. I spent about two and a half years developing the idea, creating a business plan, seeking financing, and finally opening the doors. Along the way, I brought in my wife, who had experience with the cultural center, and we combined the two ideas to create a unique concept. Raices has been incredibly well-received and has won numerous awards for its concept and beers. It continues to be recognized as a positive force in the Colorado and Denver communities.

As I progressed through different stages of education and work, I realized that each level presented its own challenges. What seemed difficult in elementary school became easier in middle school, and what seemed challenging in high school became manageable in college. Similarly, when I started working, I realized that college was relatively easier. And when I ventured into entrepreneurship, I discovered that working for someone else was comparatively simpler. As I reflect on all the different levels that I've experienced, there is value in recognizing progression. It reminds me of where I started and all that I've overcome to be in a position to be self-employed running a business that I'm truly passionate about. Our progression is our receipt that we're aligned. It's also a reminder to continue focusing on your why because your progression is proof that your why has helped you overcome all the challenges. Each level came down to one thing - hard work. Nothing beats grit and hard work in whatever level of life that you are in. Hard work will win every time, it doesn't lie, and it will always be the answer to get to the next venture and level you are seeking.

I won't lie, the prospect of having one's own business seems like a very lucid plan, yet it is riddled with surprises and challenges at every turn, and it is not for the faint of heart. Having a business is often compared to chasing a dream. Both take hard work, perseverance, time, sacrifice, and some might say, a touch of madness. I concur. If you're okay with these things and understand that your love life, family, finances, and friendships may be affected, then, proceed. There are ways to minimize these effects with enough due diligence, networking, humility, and tenacity. My advice to you is, before you make plans, ask yourself the most important thing: What makes you happy? Then, become unstoppable, like the sea.

TAMIL MALDONADO VEGA

Co-Founder & Chief Operating Officer,
Raíces Brewing Company | CULTURA

Tamil is a Latinoamericana, Caribeña, from La Isla del Encanto, Puerto Rico. She studied Computational Mathematics in PR, Applied Mathematics in AZ, and Atmospheric Sciences in DC. She loves education and experienced different educational levels as a high school and charter school teacher, a college professor, and a university professor. She has been a leader in CO, DC, AZ, and Puerto Rico. From creations of organizations along her journey to activism through self-managed organizations, she has been active in science associations, and community, artistic, and cultural organizations. She is the Co-Founder & COO of Raíces Brewing Company and serves as the Executive Director of CULTURA organization.

Opening The Door

I was born and raised in the vibrant town of Humacao, nestled on the enchanting east coast of Puerto Rico. From the moment I took my first breath, I was immersed in a world where hurricanes were not just a weather phenomenon, but integral parts of our lives, symbolizing the struggles we faced. Raised by extraordinary parents, each a leader in their own unique way, I witnessed the transformative power of their actions.

My father revolutionized Catholicism in our neighborhood by introducing Spanish as the language of worship instead of Latin. He composed religious songs in Spanish and challenged prejudice and injustice. He built relationships with pastors from other Christian churches and worked towards normalizing marriage in the priesthood. He also worked as a teacher for 30 years, making a difference in the lives of his students.

Meanwhile, my mother embarked on a remarkable journey, working as a Social Worker while studying for her master's degree in Puerto Rico. Later, she earned her Ph.D. in Social Work and received the Excellence in Research Award from New York. Her accomplishments inspired me, especially after learning about the struggles and discrimination she faced while studying overseas. She became a revered professor at the University of Puerto Rico, conducting a Master students thesis on community issues/actions on the island. She was well-known and highly respected in our town, self-managed community organizations, her workplace, and her neighborhood. I aspired to be like her - a respected and wise woman who believed in creating a positive impact.

Growing up, my extended family lived close by. We saw each other every day, and our humble abode became a sanctuary where no door was ever closed. The spirit of inclusivity and communal support thrived within our walls. Nothing I had was ever only mine, it was always for the whole family and for the neighborhood, and that went for everyone in the family. Nobody ever thought of just themselves, it was always about the family, the neighborhood, the community.

My house was an open house for the community throughout the year. My parents started a summer camp for children in our home for the neighborhood, transforming every room of our home into a vibrant summer camp. Each room of our house became an activity room, and always with all the doors open. I remember watching all the children and adults walking through the house, helping each other, learning, and always developing skills while having fun. My grandmother's house was connected to my home by a simple hall in between, and her kitchen was the kitchen for the camp where she and other adults and seniors of the community cooked for the children breakfast and lunch. My father created the neighborhood children's chorale and my mom drafted and reviewed documents that identified struggles happening in the community while providing a voice for individuals to effectively present issues. At other times we were heading to community meetings, conferences, workshops, professional development activities or social events. These formative experiences instilled in me a deep appreciation for the power of community, shaping the very foundation upon which I built my life.

When my mother left for New York to get her Ph.D., I was ten years old. Despite the difficulty of being without her for two years, I never felt lonely or alone. My family, neighbors, and community always made me feel loved and supported. This feeling has influenced my work, as I strive to recreate that sense of warmth and love for others. Our family prioritized uplifting and improving the lives of others, rather than material possessions or personal gain. I have vivid memories of our community coming together to make

Puerto Rican pasteles to raise funds for my mother's studies. This collective effort allowed her dreams to come true and had a profound impact on me. It instilled in me a belief that we all have a responsibility to help one another. With every step I take, I choose to develop projects that benefit the community and activate spaces that have a positive impact. I have experienced the power of collective effort and understand that every small or large contribution brings us closer to achieving our goals.

Despite the poverty that enveloped our neighborhood, my parents, armed with the invaluable gift of a college education, developed skills and knowledge that could benefit our neighborhood, our city, and our island, and they selflessly utilized every ounce of what they had to devise innovative solutions that would enhance the quality of life for our beloved community and people. They were passionate advocates for education, constantly seeking solutions and fighting for change within the system. I was raised to actively participate in movements, dedicating our weekends to standing up for our rights and the rights of others, and voicing concerns about abuse and injustice towards human rights in any shape or form. Human rights became a core value, as I understood that they were not just privileges, but fundamental to the dignity of humanity.

After high school, I knew that I wanted to continue my parents' path and attend college. With both of my parents being educators, I understood the fundamental importance of getting a college education. However, I knew that I didn't want to venture outside of my hometown and specifically my home, which I knew I wasn't quite ready for as I still desired to remain close to my family. As a result, I turned my attention to an area that interested me- computational mathematics. I've always been the type of person who strives to accomplish the seemingly impossible. Even if something appears to be unattainable, I am determined to give it my best shot. I figure that if I fail, I won't dwell on it, but rather accept it and move on, but at least I tried. Obtaining my bachelor's in computational mathematics proved to be the ultimate challenge for me. We didn't have internet or a computer at home when I started, so I had to use the computers at the university, and I would often stay until two or three in the morning to finish my schoolwork with colleagues. My dad would bring me food made by someone in my family and would wait for me patiently until I was done with my projects.

I dedicated myself to my studies and to getting actively involved in the institution in leadership positions, and was Student Senate Representative for two years, and the reactivator and president of the Computational Mathematics Students Association. I loved every minute of it! Every summer break, I eagerly engaged in research activities. I delved into the realms of physics and astronomy for a period and subsequently immersed myself in applied mathematics under the guidance of another esteemed professor for the final two years. These endeavors broadened my horizons and pushed me to explore beyond the confines of my comfort zone. I felt empowered and knew that I was now ready to spread my wings farther and discover the world. I started applying to big universities in the United States and felt confident when I accepted an invitation from Arizona State University to visit their campus. I was invited to visit the University during the Spring Break before I started my academic year. They generously covered the expenses for my hotel stay during the week-long visit. It seemed that only ten people were invited, and I was the only Latino/Latina representation among them. Upon arrival, I was asked if I knew English, which surprised me. When I confirmed that I did, they mentioned that my performance on the English test (TOEFL) was not impressive. I smiled and explained that the TOEFL focuses more on technical aspects of the language rather than conversational skills, to which we are not necessarily exposed extensively in Puerto Rico. I was grateful that despite their hidden concerns before I visited, they still invited me based on my academic achievements. I must confess that this is not the only time in my life that people have provided a chance for me (knowingly or not), that has elevated my opportunities in life, and that has reinforced me to pay it forward by taking a chance on others and looking for ways to provide opportunities for others.

Moving to the United States was a significant cultural shift for me, and it felt like I was starting from scratch. Not only did I leave my family and my country, but I also had to adjust to a new environment where everyone spoke English. I had no friends or network and had little understanding of North American culture. Additionally, I was the only Latina in my master's degree program. I couldn't find any university clubs or organizations specifically for Latino or Hispanic individuals. This made me question why there was a lack of representation. I noticed that many Latinos were working in maintenance and construction roles on campus, but not as many pursuing higher education. It led me to wonder about the barriers and challenges they may face in accessing education. It became important to me to advocate for more opportunities for Latinos in education and to address the various factors that may limit their access, such as status, financial constraints, lack of support, and the need to prioritize work and family responsibilities. I recognized that I was fortunate to receive the privilege and provided resources through an assistantship grant by the university to pursue higher education, and I wanted to help create more opportunities for other Latinos in the United States who may face more restrictions and limitations. I started actively getting involved on campus, searching for other Latinos who may feel the same way I do. After graduating with a Master of Science degree, I completed my teaching practice at Tempe High School. Teaching and helping others advance educationally felt like the right path for me. I stayed in Arizona to gain more teaching experience, working at various levels and educational systems. This allowed me to understand the challenges faced by our Latino population in each institution and provide support for their success.

It took time to get accustomed to how people interacted with one another. Fortunately, I was able to meet and make two new friends at church, one from Venezuela and the other from Ecuador. It was comforting to have a community that shared a similar cultural identity and understood the warmth and approachability that I was accustomed to. Through all of this, I had to maintain a balance between my studies and life, so every weekend I went out dancing to my Latin music. Through dancing to Caribbean music, I was able to relieve the pressures and stress of the mental work that I was involved in and stay connected to my culture.

Eventually, I returned to Puerto Rico and became a professor at the University of Puerto Rico, where I had previously completed my bachelor's degree. It was a full-circle moment for me and felt amazing to see how my journey had come back to where it all started. I felt a sense of accomplishment and fulfillment knowing that I had achieved my goals and had the opportunity to give back to the University of Puerto Rico as a professor. During my time as a professor, my friend (and my undergraduate research colleague) was pursuing a PhD in atmospheric science at Howard University. They needed someone to join their research groups, and since I had previous research experience and was already a professor with a master's degree in applied mathematics, my colleague asked if I wanted to go. She spoke to her advisor about my qualifications, and I was given the opportunity to join the research cruises. Call it fate, but interestingly enough there was another ticket that became available that was given to a student at Howard University, who later became my husband, José, who is also a co-author in this book.

After such an unexpected opportunity, it opened the doors for me to go to Washington D.C. and start studying Atmospheric Sciences. During my time at the institution, I looked for ways to provide a voice, build community among students, and create opportunities. I was able to participate and create many accomplishments that had an impact on the world and community around me. On the other hand, I was evolving in my personal life and got married in 2009.

In 2011, I did an internship in Colorado and loved the state, the tranquility, and the connection to nature. Due to the political climate against undocumented immigrants in the D.C. area, José and I decided to move to Colorado to start a family. I couldn't find any cultural organizations that represented my identity, so I co-founded Barrio E' Centro to promote Latino Arts and Culture. We offered Bomba drum and dance classes, engaged the community in cultural workshops, performed in festivals, and organized the Colorado Latino Festival. I also worked with Latino/Latina students in High Schools through the YWCA to develop educational and cultural programming. The goal was to share and value our people and culture while promoting integration. Three years after founding Barrio E' Centro in 2012, we opened the first Multicultural Community Center in Boulder County called Barrio E' Centro in September 2015 that ran for a year and a month where we collected data of the needs of the Latino community by providing space for collaboration, culture, artists, performance, community involvement and participation through meetings, activities, and partnerships.

The same year we opened Barrio E' Centro, I gave birth to my son Ara'Ni. That same week, I also had an interview with the City Council to become an Arts Commissioner for the City of Boulder. Despite the events surrounding my pregnancy and the birth of my son, I felt a strong sense of pride as I walked in my mother's footsteps, remembering her struggles and accomplishments while pregnant with me. After the interview, I received devastating news that my mom had stage four liver cancer. I flew to see her, introduce her to her grandson, and say my final goodbyes. We discussed my community projects and the importance of not forgetting my identity and culture. Two weeks later, she passed away.

While fighting for collective benefit as an Arts Commissioner looking for ways to provide opportunities for groups and individuals within the arts fields within the grants, we provided by changing requirements that could become an obstacle for them to apply for funding, I faced a cruel reality in my personal life. I struggled to find a place to live with my new family of three because apartment management required all members to have a social security number, which my husband did not have as an undocumented immigrant. I advocated for change by presenting my case to the Human Relations Commission and City Council, highlighting the housing restrictions that affected not only undocumented individuals but also citizens like me and my son. I drew upon my upbringing in activism and my role as a protective mother and wife to fight for our right to live as a united family in the city where we worked and contributed.

The history of the West side of the United States differs from the East side, with a history of land appropriation and changing borders. The media often presents a uniform message, but the reality is that the West side has a different story. Many families on the East Coast were invited to come to the United States for work, such as in agriculture or manufacturing. However, there is now a negative narrative that portrays immigrants as invaders, which ignores their contributions. Hispanic and Latino communities face mistreatment and lack of access to education and resources due to the lack of understanding about the history and our value which is concerning as they are all part of how we are becoming increasingly important in the workforce. The words society uses does matter and it affects how people feel individually and collectively. Researching and learning about true history and the impact of words can open doors for better understanding. Mistreating and devaluing people based on misinformation or lack of understanding is unjust and creates a negative impact on society. The polarization in our country's politics adds to the challenges we face in treating each other with humanity. This mistreatment affects people's opportunities and sense of belonging. Empowerment in the Latino community is needed to rectify this problem.

My husband and I opened Raíces Brewing Company, a community-cultural-resource center that supports the Latino community. We provide visibility to artists and small vendors, offer job opportunities, and create programming to reinforce knowledge and pride in our heritage. Our space is a symbiotic relationship with the community, connecting people and developing leadership skills. For example, if someone asks about a book club, we offer them the opportunity to become a leader and activate one through our organization, even if they have no prior experience. We assure them that we will provide support and resources, including our space and designated meeting times, and will assist with visuals and promotion at no cost. Our book club was created two years ago, only focused on Latino authors, and it now has 273 members.

Sometimes, people hesitate to take risks and create opportunities for others, but it is crucial to remember that we wouldn't be where we are today if others hadn't taken a chance on us. At Raíces Brewing Company, one of our main struggles was the financial aspect. As the three co-founders, José, Martín, and myself, none of us came from wealthy backgrounds. We didn't have family or friends who could provide financial support, so we had to build our network from scratch. When we were looking for partners and investors, we faced skepticism because we were relatively unknown and didn't have established connections. However, there were people who believed in us and took a risk by supporting our vision. Providing an opportunity and opening a door to one individual can have a significant impact and potentially rectify generations of social injustices within an entire family, an entire community, and an entire ethnic group! If more people are willing to take such risks and support others, we can create more opportunities for every-one, creating a domino effect of positive massive impact in our society. Let's continue opening doors!

JERRY NATIVIDAD

Chief Executive Officer,
Emeritus

Jerry is a highly involved member of his community, both locally and nationally. He founded the Commission on Cultural Diversity and Human Relations for the City of Lakewood in 1991 and co-founded the Colorado Hispanic League. Jerry has served in various roles and organizations, including the Lakewood Legacy Foundation, Leadership Council for Better Education in Jefferson County, Denver Urban Renewal Authority, University of Colorado - School of Business, small business council - Denver Metro Chamber of Commerce, Governor's Minority Business Office, and Governor Owens' Transition team. He was appointed to the National Advisory Council for the Small Business Administration and serves on the advisory board of the Latino Coalition. In 2016, Jerry ran for the United States Senate as a candidate in the Republican primary.

A Tapestry of Heritage, Curiosity, And Extending a Helping Hand

My grandfather, a Filipino by birth, embarked on a remarkable journey that spanned continents. From the shores of the Philippines, he ventured to Mexico, seeking new opportunities and experiences. It was in this vibrant country that he found himself, embracing the Mexican culture, marrying my grandmother, and forging connections that would shape his future. Driven by his thirst for opportunity, my grandfather eventually set his sights on southeastern Colorado, a land brimming with promise and untapped potential. It was here, amidst the vast expanse of fertile fields and boundless skies, that he decided to lay down roots and build a life for himself.

As fate would have it, my father, a product of this unique blend of Filipino and Mexican heritage, was born in the United States, specifically in the enchanting state of New Mexico. The juxtaposition of cultures and traditions that coursed through his veins created a captivating tapestry of identity, one that would later be passed down to me and my siblings. Growing up in a tight-knit farming community, our family was intimately acquainted with the ebb and flow of rural life. With less than 400 individuals comprising our community, the bonds we formed were deep-rooted and enduring. It was within this nurturing environment that my inquisitive nature flourished, fueled by the encouragement of my loved ones. My older sister, Gloria, who has since departed this world, often marveled at my boundless energy and insatiable thirst for knowledge. She would affectionately jest, wondering aloud what the future held for someone as endlessly curious as me. It was through their unwavering support and belief in my potential that I learned to embrace my innate curiosity and unyielding spirit.

In elementary school, during the 1950's, I was learning to read, when a significant incident unfolded that would forever be etched in my memory. It was my very first experience with discrimination and understanding race and culture. Every day, on my way to and from school, my sister and I would pass by a restaurant on Main Street called Rancher's Restaurant. It was during one of these walks home that I stumbled upon a sign that read, "No Mexicans or dogs allowed." I'm around nine years old and these are some of the first words I read. The words struck me with a mix of confusion and curiosity. I couldn't help but stare at the sign, my sister urging me to keep moving. It wasn't until the weekend, during a breakfast conversation with my parents, that I mustered the courage to bring up what I had read. I asked my dad if I had misread the sign, repeating the words, "No Mexicans or dogs allowed." His reaction was a mixture of surprise and pride in my growing reading abilities. However, he quickly realized that I understood the implications behind those words. Looking at my mom, he acknowledged the weight of the situation. At that moment, my dad chose to handle the situation with grace and wisdom. He explained to me that the sign meant that the restaurant did not want people like us, Mexicans, to enter. But instead of dwelling on the exclusion, he shifted the focus to the power we held as a family. He emphasized that the money we earned could be spent elsewhere, where doors would be open to us. We didn't have to enter a place that didn't welcome us. His answer stayed with me throughout my life. It is what we choose to focus on that matters, and we all have a choice to choose.

Oddly enough, in the tight-knit farming community I grew up in, racism seemed to be absent. I vividly remember accompanying my father, Sammy, to the post office located next to the restaurant. Every Saturday, as he collected the mail, we would encounter ranchers exiting the establishment. These ranchers, all of them Caucasian, would warmly greet my father, asking about our family and showing genuine interest in my well-being. They even invited me to ride horses with them. In that moment, the significance of the "Mexicans and dogs not allowed" sign eluded me. I was more focused on the dogs and why they weren't allowed inside, because I was shielded from the racial implications of such a sign. However, I didn't understand why friends of my father's would still be in the restaurant that didn't allow us in it.

Years later, the topic resurfaced during a conversation with my family. My Aunt Nellie had worked at a restaurant nearby, and I noticed the absence of a discriminatory sign there. It was then that my father shared a profound insight that has stayed with me ever since. He acknowledged our Mexican heritage with pride, emphasizing our strong work ethic. He explained that while the ranchers and farmers who frequented the restaurant were not responsible for the sign, they still chose to dine there. In our small farming community, my father believed in judging individuals based on their character rather than their ethnicity or skin color. He went on to list important values for me to live my life by.

Long before Martin Luther King Jr. referenced judgment by our character rather than the color of our skin, he said to treat people with respect, if they give you a job, you work hard and show up early and stay late, if you owe money then you pay it on the day you get paid, you make sure you're honest, and that is what will bring you respect as a Mexican in this town. I've never forgotten these principles, and in fact, they have shaped my perspective and continue to guide me in life. In fact, it wasn't until later in life when I moved to Denver Colorado, I didn't understand racism.

My father's unwavering belief in the importance of education and the English language shaped my upbringing. Growing up in the 50's and early 60's, he constantly reminded me that success in this great country could only be achieved through a solid education and fluency in English because that's the language of this country. Sitting at the table with my older sister, diligently doing our homework together, we understood the discipline required to excel academically. Both my parents instilled in us the understanding that education was the key to unlocking opportunities. From elementary school to junior high and high school, I embraced this mindset. Engaging in sports, I found my passion in wrestling and excelled in baseball and track. My father was my biggest cheerleader, and while he encouraged my athletic pursuits, he reminded me that to participate in sports, my grades must continue to remain good otherwise he'd pull me out. He emphasized that education always came first, reminding me to strive to be the best version of myself in the classroom and as a person. He never pressured me to be the smartest person in the room, but rather to focus on personal growth, discipline, and respect for authority. With my father's guidance, I navigated high school successfully, maintaining a strong GPA that reflected my dedication to my studies. While perfection was not the goal, I understood the importance of a solid academic foundation for my future endeavors.

Growing up in a hardworking family, I was not fully aware of the struggles we faced. My parents, both my dad and mom, worked tirelessly to provide for our family. Even at a young age, around nine or ten years old, I began to contribute by working in the fields alongside my aunt and uncle. While my mom took care of other responsibilities and worked to support our family, my dad took on multiple roles, working multiple jobs. Contributing as well, my older sister and I would join my aunt's crew, planting and harvesting produce, doing the work that migrant farmworkers typically do. Although I was not supposed to be out in the fields at my age, my aunt Antonia would bring me along because I insisted on being a part of it. She had a good relationship with the farmers, so they allowed me to join as long as I didn't get too much sun exposure. Looking back at our family unit, I never saw us stressing over anything. We always had enough to eat, and I don't recall ever going hungry. The only time I questioned our circumstances was during Thanksgiving when everyone and many of my Anglo friends talked about having turkey while we had chicken. I asked my dad why we couldn't have a turkey like everyone else, and he explained that a chicken was what we could afford. He emphasized that there was no real difference between a turkey and a chicken, except that turkeys were bigger. I accepted his explanation without complaint, realizing that our circumstances were different from others. We as a family always appreciated what we had in hand, we always gave thanks and were happy as a Mexican family in this small town.

I never felt a sense of poverty growing up. I've gone back to visit the home and neighborhood I lived in as a child and brought my wife, daughter, and granddaughters with me. My family was amazed at this tiny three - room house and its simplicity because, to them, it looked like a house for a poverty-stricken family. Yet, for me, it was a reminder of all the wonderful memories I had with my family. I always remind them that it's not the size or appearance of a house that matters, but the love and memories that are created within its walls. It didn't matter where we lived either, the warmth that I felt at any place we lived, is because of the memories we shared. When I was fifteen years old, we had to move to another small town nearby called Rocky Ford, which now has a population of 4,000 people. It was around this time that the Chicano movement was gaining momentum, and I found myself attending a meeting out of curiosity with a few of my friends from my school. However, my father found out and sat me down and expressed his disapproval. He emphasized the importance of focusing on being proud of being American and prioritizing my education. He made it clear that getting involved in the Chicano power movement would only serve as a distraction and hinder my future possibilities. While my friends were actively participating in various activities, I chose to remain on the sidelines, not disclosing the true reason behind my decision. My father's sternness and seriousness on this matter left a lasting impression on me. More importantly, he emphasized that we were proud Mexicans and the word Chicano was divisive and implied that the world was racist, and going back to my upbringing as a young child I remember it is about me, not them. He urged me to concentrate on myself, my education, and the endless possibilities that lay ahead. He believed that I had the potential to become anything I wanted, whether it be a lawyer, a doctor, or a successful business owner. He encouraged me to stay focused on my studies and excel in my athletic pursuits.

In high school, my father would always make me sit down with him at the dinner table after dinner. He wanted me to go through my day and share what I learned in school. At first, I didn't understand why he was making me do this. I thought maybe he didn't trust me or something. But then he told me that he was getting his education through me. He explained that he was learning from everything I was learning and that it was important to him. This revelation made me emotional, and from that day forward, I looked forward to coming home and sharing my day with him. He became very involved in my education, working closely with me and even learning alongside me. I would tell him about the books I was reading and the math problems I was solving, and he was always interested and supportive. He was a smart guy, and I cherished the moments we shared discussing my schoolwork. My father laid a strong foundation for me and our family, and I credit him for any success I have in my life.

He always emphasized the importance of character, quality, honesty, and determination. He taught me that being a good person is what truly matters. This strict yet purposeful upbringing shaped my worldview and instilled in me a strong sense of direction. Thanks to my parents' strict upbringing and emphasis on education, I maintained a disciplined lifestyle throughout high school. This dedication paid off when I was awarded a full scholarship to Oklahoma State University Stillwater, Oklahoma. I was the first person in my family to attend college, where I pursued a bachelor's degree. Although I wasn't a first-team wrestler, I was grateful for the opportunity to be part of the team and have a full-ride scholarship. While attending a university in a different state, I found myself in a predominantly white environment. Although I didn't experience racism, I was aware of my differences and knew that I had to work hard and stay focused on my future.

After I got my Bachelor of Science degree in Business, I returned to Rocky Ford, my dad greeted me with a puzzled look instead of a warm hug and congratulations. He immediately asked me why I was there, and I jokingly replied that I was just visiting. He then questioned whether I planned to stay in the small farming community or take my degree elsewhere. It hadn't occurred to me before, but he was right. What could I do with a bachelor's degree in a place dominated by farms? Thanks to my father's political connections, I ended up working for the county government and Governor Lamm in Denver. My dad played a significant role in opening those doors for me. Moving to Denver was a way to escape Rocky Ford, and I took the opportunity even though it wasn't my original plan. Because my father understood politics and I learned from him, I accepted the position in the Governor's office with my eye on how this could work for my future.

My father passed away at the young age of fifty-six. It was devastating for me because we were very close. After he was gone, I turned to my sister and expressed my confusion, saying, "I don't understand why I'm doing this, because dad isn't here anymore." "I can be honest with you." She said, "He would be incredibly proud of what you, my brother, have achieved. You see, he was living vicariously through you. Your accomplishments are a reflection of his unfulfilled aspirations, and he instilled in you the drive to accomplish everything he wished he could have."

My original intention was never to stay in politics or work for the government. After resigning from the governor's office, I found myself without a job. However, I had the opportunity to meet Ward Kelly, a former state senator and contractor. He proposed starting a new business venture together and offered to support it for three years. Despite my lack of knowledge in manufacturing, Ward took me under his wing and became a mentor figure in my life. Ward was an Anglo man, yet unlike what many would expect, he never referenced my race, but only pointed out my enthusiasm and drive success. He almost became like a second father to me. We developed a strong friendship and eventually became partners. Unfortunately, he passed away not long after that. Losing both my father and Ward was tough, but their influence laid a strong foundation for my success today. If I achieve success in my life, I commit to giving back. I believe in sending the elevator back down and opening doors for others who want to achieve greatness. This can be through mentorship, encouragement, or financial assistance. In 2016, I ran for the United States Senate, and although I was not successful, I knew my dad would be proud. I wanted to make a difference for my daughter, granddaughters, and all the youth of America.

In 1989, my wife and I started our own company, which has been incredibly successful. We now have nearly 2,000 employees across the United States. Now in semi-retirement, my daughter and granddaughter are taking over the company. I continue to speak at events and share my experiences on achieving success in life. I have also been involved in giving back to the community where I grew up. I helped rebuild the high school I attended and assisted in obtaining a grant to convert it into a K-12 learning center. I paid for the consulting work myself to ensure the school district could receive the grant. I share these stories because I never forget where I came from. Just like my father taught me, I don't focus on racism or discrimination. I am blessed with a supportive wife, a wonderful daughter, two incredible granddaughters, and great friends. Being Mexican American doesn't hinder my life. The challenge arises when one believes that being Mexican brings trouble. As I think back to that sign of no dogs or Mexicans allowed, I realize the power of the dollar and how my family controls our destiny.

We are drivers of America's economy. God put you on this earth to succeed, regardless of your skin color or heritage. Don't be sidelined by politics. Walk proud with those dollar bills in your hand.

EDUCATION, NON-PROFITS & ERGs

GIL JUAREZ

Co-Author

Gil Juarez, from San Diego, California, was raised by a single parent, became a U.S.MC Reservist in 1985, an infantry officer in 1995, and rose to the rank of Colonel. Over his 39-year career, he commanded from the small team to the infantry regiment. While a Marine Captain he deployed in support of Operation Iraqi Freedom as company commander, Charlie Company, 1st Light Armored Reconnaissance Battalion, and participated in Operation Opening Gambit, Task Force Tripoli, and Operation New Dawn (Al Fallujah). He holds three master's degrees including a Masters of Executive Leadership from U.S.C. His personal awards include the Defense Superior Service Medal, the Legion of Merit, Bronze Star with Valor device, the Meritorious Service Medal with 3 Gold Stars, the Navy and Marine Corps Commendation Medal with Gold Star and Valor device, the Navy and Marine Corps Achievement Medal, and the Combat Action Ribbon.

Finding a Path to the "Good Life"

After thirty-nine years of Marine Corps service, combat, and multiple command tours, you might expect to read about character development from a military perspective. Character forms long before one enters combat, through an iterative process of reflection, acceptance, and action. This chapter concentrates on elements of my life we are more likely to have in common with the hope it inspires action toward the only thing you control yourself. This story represents my opinions and does not reflect the policies of the Department of Defense, or United States Marine Corps. This chapter is a distillation of my memories and perceptions, and I apologize for any inaccuracies, which are wholly mine. I dedicate this chapter to my loving wife, and my mother, the strongest women I know.

The Stoics aimed to live a virtuous or the "good life," to achieve tranquility. According to Epictetus, tranquility begins with, "Demand not that events should happen as you wish; but wish them to happen as they do happen, and you will go on well." These are the events as they happened to me and through me, I am grateful for each.

My mom, Esther, starting at age seventeen, quit high school, married, and quickly thereafter gave birth to my three older siblings. She, still very young, divorced her husband to protect her children from his drug use. A few years later, me, then my sister were born. While dating my father, my mom announced she was pregnant and he announced he had a family, and they separated. Later, my mother skeptical of men and hyper-protective of her children, also refused to marry my sister's father to shield us from his growing substance abuse.

Our family lived on welfare, and three boys split a room in our low-income apartment in the border town of San Ysidro, California. Mom did under-the-table cleaning jobs so she could save money to buy us new clothes and shoes each school year while she walked around with holes on the bottom of her shoes. Despite not having a high school diploma, her grit, natural intelligence, and work ethic allowed her to go from dishwasher in schools and hospitals, to a management position at a retirement home where she worked for over eighteen years. Now in her 80's and after all she has endured, I have never heard her complain. She remains grounded, lovingly tough, brutally honest, and eternally positive - a true Stoic warrior.

"The child who is not embraced by the village will burn it down to feel its warmth." – African proverb

Our neighborhood was poor, and as the years progressed, gangs became more violent and drugs more prevalent. I saw my first death at eight, an elderly man was hit and drug over a block by a doped-up lowrider, and at ten, outside my bedroom window, a drug deal went bad and a boy was shot in the face. Despite the occasional exposure to the ugly side, we had plenty of fun and adventure-filled moments and I had a loving family, grandparents, aunts and uncles, cousins, and friends.

At age nine my mother remarried a toxic, hyper-negative, foul-mouthed, racist, control freak who was challenged by my sibling's growing independence. His reaction to any mistake or failure was to belittle and shame you. Speaking for myself I began to believe him; insecurity took root and it took me years to regain my confidence. Luckily, he was a commercial fisherman and would be at sea for months, providing all of us long respites.

I believe my brothers and sisters sought refuge by quitting school, joining gangs, or using drugs. In time, our family lost contact with my oldest sister due to her crystal-meth addiction; thankfully, she is in recovery and in contact with my mom. In 2019, my older brother, after repeated incarcerations, and heroin addiction, hung himself in prison. I love and miss them dearly, and their addiction and suffering linger with me still.

I have often been asked how I overcame the many obstacles and there are a few factors. A loving and strong mother, moving prior to ninth grade to a middle-class neighborhood, Chula Vista, CA, joining the cross-country team, finding a good group of friends and neighbors that became family, and becoming a Marine.

Mom demonstrated great selflessness. I once asked, "Why don't you leave him?" She replied, "Because I am not sure how I can take care of you kids." That cut me like a sharp knife, and I encouraged her to leave while committing to honor her sacrifice. She remained with my stepdad into my college years, until he was incarcerated for robbing a bank which cemented an overdue separation. Her example is a source of my mental toughness - if she could endure all that, why can't I endure some inconvenience or petty problem?

My mom's indomitable and loving spirit is accompanied by a hard-hitting frankness. While struggling in college and feeling a little sorry for myself, I expressed dissatisfaction and my perception she was spending more time and energy on my siblings than on me. Her words hit like a punch of truth to the face, "Gil, they need me now more than you, and I know you can take care of yourself." I felt small, she was doing triage and was right, I was not a victim and could solve my own problems - it was a seminal moment that shaped my perspective forever.

Besides being insecure, I felt like a fish out of water in the middle-class school setting. As a younger boy, I never participated in team activities. By tenth grade, I was a poor physical specimen and thought joining the cross-country team would be a good solution. On the first day, coach Ian Cummings instructed me to run a mile.

Completely exhausted after half a mile, I was ready to quit. A thirty-second exchange ensued and became one of the most important moments of my life.

Coach called me over, looked me in the eye, and said, "If you quit today, you'll quit every other hard day of your life. I hope you come back tomorrow." His reaction was the opposite of what my stepdad would have done. He didn't ridicule, or scold, he was honest yet supportive. I did come back and by my senior year, I was a top-ten league champion. More importantly, through the team, I met incredible friends, who helped me get to the graduation finish line. The cross-country and track teams were also the first settings where I was recognized as inspirational, and "most motivational" teammate and I began to recognize where my strengths lie.

I wasn't a model student however and had my fair share of negative behaviors, like binge drinking. Alcohol was a crutch, a way to feel confident and to fit in. Just before graduation I was in a drunk driving accident and arrested. Luckily, I was the only one hurt. My advantages through high school were I loved learning and had good friends, who were good students - this combination kept me in school.

Simultaneously, another powerful force was shaping me in ways I didn't even know. The best part of our move was the neighbors, Mark and Melissa Carman, a gift from God. The Carmans, a young 20ish couple, devout Christians, just had their first of two children. Melissa a receptionist, and Mark a cabinet maker opened their home, extended family, and their lives to me. I spent hours learning woodworking from Mark, helped him with yard projects, and discussed all manner of religious, philosophical, and life topics at their dinner table.

When my parents temporarily separated during high school, we lost the house, and my mom and sisters went to stay with my grandparents. Their home was small, and far away, so the Carmans took me in that semester. Being with them pre-, post, and during this phase of life exposed me to what a stable family could be, and I reflected on their example many times in my own family journey. The Carmans continue to be a big brother and sister, I love them dearly.

Towards the end of high school, my parents fought frequently, and my relationship with my stepfather grew worse. I never yearned for a different life or thought life was bad but during one major fight between my parents, I remember considering suicide. It was the only time I ever had suicidal thoughts and my response was to focus on the positive things such as school, running, and friends.

I discovered a few things my senior year, I was fit, a natural leader, and I wanted to attend college, yet I didn't know how or have the means. My great-uncles were WWII Marines, my best friend's Dad, Mr. Dixon, had been a Marine, and I had a high school friend who recently joined. The idea of joining the Marine Corps offered me the opportunity to gain discipline, confidence, and some college money, so I signed up for the Marine Reserves on December 7th, 1984. I consider this decision and that of marrying my wife *two* of the *three* best and most important decisions I ever made. I credit the Marine Corps for putting my life on a path of good and service to others, though I still veered astray for a while.

I was in the reserves for nearly ten years, as I muddled my way through college and life. I, the wet-behind-the-ears eighteen-year-old, was now surrounded by peers who were business owners, professionals, police officers, detectives, and a few Vietnam veterans. Though close in rank, many were older than me, which allowed me to learn from their life and family experiences. A significant role model and friend I met in the unit and who enabled my journey was Scott Wells.

Scott was planning to become an officer, but his dad had health problems and Scott made the difficult decision to take over the family business. We not only served together nine plus years, he provided a starving student with a place to live at a discounted rate for over six years. I will be eternally grateful and respectful of a man whose decision to put family first defines virtue.

As a Marine, I was excelling and growing at a rapid rate while I also worked as a janitor, a meatpacking worker, at McDonald's, and Home Depot to get through college. I oscillated between full-time and part-time college and work, and some semesters did both full-time. I was on the path of becoming an adaptive physical education teacher and had no plans to become an officer. Three influential men however would alter that plan.

Midway through my reserve career, Gunnery Sergeant Robles, a prior active-duty Marine, had taken me under his wing. Gunny asked me what I enjoyed about being a Marine. I told him I loved the responsibility, the training, and taking care of Marines. He explained that as an officer, I would have the ability to set policy and give guidance to entire commands which is a way to take care of Marines at a larger scale. He thought teaching wouldn't satisfy me and he encouraged me to become an officer. Similarly, another agent of change, Art Stone, my community college mentor in the physical education department was also shaping me. Art was one of those teachers who connected with students and took an interest in their lives, and he encouraged me to become an officer. To be honest, I was scared about the responsibility and wasn't sure I was up to the task.

It was in my final years at San Diego State University that Gunny Robles was killed in a motorcycle accident. His loss hit me hard and was a catalyst for me making the third most important decision of my life, earning my commission. I carried Gunny's memorial service program with me through Officer Candidates School and every other step of my Marine Corps journey. He has never left my side, in training or combat, I hope I made him proud. It was about this time I met what would become one of my closest friends, Captain Todd Buechs.

Todd was an infantry and reconnaissance Marine, a Naval Academy graduate, an Officer Selection Officer (recruiter) in San Diego, CA, and a man of incredible character and discipline. He would be a role model, a mentor, and to this day, a brother. I was walking across campus and like young Marines do, sticking out of the crowd, and we struck up a conversation at his recruiting table. Soon I was helping train his officer candidates, and we worked out together several times a week. I thought life had finally turned in the right direction, I was excelling at school, I was a respected Staff Sergeant in the Marine Reserves, and I submitted my application to Officer Candidate School.

Unfortunately, I was not selected because I had a DUI arrest, a marijuana waiver, and a tattoo waiver on my application. Despite nearly eight years of faithful service, the denial was a hard blow. I felt ashamed but I couldn't change it, I could only go forward. Unbeknownst to me, Todd stuck his neck out for me and advocated my case to his commanding officer, and I was approved. I vowed to repay his and Gunny Robles' faith by doing my best as an officer candidate and officer, I have since viewed my career as an opportunity to pay it back as well as forward.

My insecurities and dysfunctions did not end in the social, work, and academic spheres, it permeated my relations with the opposite sex. I was a wreck in so many ways, unwilling to commit, and self-ish. Alcohol plagued my relations and though I accept full accountability for all acts and failures, alcohol was a willing and enabling passenger. Luckily, after many broken relations, and before commissioning I started dating my soul mate.

Cyndi and I worked together years before at Home Depot. When we were reacquainted, she had been through a horrible divorce, was a single mom, raising three kids, and trying to make it on her own. She is an immensely kind, loving, intelligent, and strong person. We soon realized we were in love, and that we wanted a chance at something different. We married quickly, and before you knew it she was pregnant, and making our first household move alone, while I was on deployment.

We both wanted a successful marriage, yet we struggled to achieve it. We came from dysfunctional families and were probably codependent. I was focused on doing things my way and was never home. To add insult to injury, marrying a Marine resulted in her losing equal custody of the kids. We were in debt, living paycheck to paycheck, miserable, and on the verge of divorce.

I knew we were failing and that I needed to change something. While driving home I recalled to myself why I loved and married her. I then added up my own inadequacies and acknowledged trying to change her while taking no action for myself. I was immature, a workaholic, and a poor communicator. I thought of the Carmans, of Todd and Karla Buechs, and the words of my coach, "If you quit today, you will quit every other hard day of your life." I realized the only thing I controlled was myself and that I would not allow our marriage to fail because I quit or failed to try.

My new enduring *mission* became to be a better teammate to my wife and marriage. It sounds unreal but at that moment it felt like a great weight had been lifted and our marriage began an immediate turn for the good. Even though I had more growing to do I made a major leap toward living the "good life."

"The obstacle in the way, becomes the way." – Marcus Aurelius

During these formative years, I learned profound lessons. I discovered that every challenge is also an opportunity for personal growth. That failure is not something to be feared or avoided, but rather a companion to growth. That you don't have to do it alone and that you are truly only in control of one thing – your reaction to the uncertainties and challenges of life.

Furthermore, I firmly believe that our attitude and mindset play a crucial role in shaping our experiences. I have come to realize that we have the power to choose between being miserable or positive in any given situation. By consciously choosing positivity, we open ourselves up to a world of possibilities and create an environment conducive to personal and professional growth.

This requires a certain level of vulnerability and a willingness to step outside of our comfort zones. By embracing these qualities, I have been able to embark on new adventures, take risks, and expand my horizons. Lastly, I firmly believe that we are not meant to navigate this journey called life alone. We are interconnected beings, and our success and fulfillment are often intertwined with the support and collaboration of others. This realization has led me to adopt the mantra of "Mission, Team, Self."

I have come to understand that everything in life falls into this triad. Whether it was my decision to join the Marines, pursue higher education, or become an officer, or be a husband, my focus has always been on the greater mission and collective success of the team. Two important U.S.MC leadership principles are key, "know yourself and seek self-improvement," and "seek responsibility and take responsibility for your actions."

In conclusion, my early years were filled with valuable lessons that have shaped my outlook on life. I have learned the importance of embracing challenges, viewing failure as an opportunity, choosing positivity, being open to growth, and recognizing the significance of selflessness and teamwork. By incorporating these principles into my life, I have been able to find a sense of purpose, fulfillment, and tranquility and I wish you the same.

MARTHA NIÑO RODRIGUEZ

Senior Silicon Valley Technology Professor | Speaker | Author

Martha Niño Rodriguez was born in central Mexico to humble parents who picked cotton. She was smuggled into the U.S.A. as a child. She was poor, she got kicked out of school but despite the obstacles, she is a 25+ year technology professional who has worked at large corporations ranging from mobile, and hardware to software. Her path to tech was never part of the future - yet, with the help of believers from different backgrounds - she is there. Her voice and story were silent. Finding power, passion, and purpose in her voice has given her a reason to continue to use her superpower – her story.

THE 5 H'S:
Hurt, Hope, Hustle, Help, Heart

When the house keys were given to me, a rush of emotions flooded my mind. It was as if a replay of my entire life flew before my mind, highlighting all the effort and sacrifices that led me to this pivotal moment. Not only had I endured countless hardships, but my parents had also faced more than their fair share of struggles. You see, my current position in life is far from what was expected of me, especially considering my humble beginnings as a young girl from Mexico. I was brought to the United States as an infant baby by a person known as a "coyote", a complete stranger entrusted by my mother with the task of safely transporting me. With nothing but faith and hope, my mother entrusted me to this stranger, believing that our journey would lead us to a better future on the other side. I can't even imagine all the things that could have gone wrong or how that must have felt for my mother. Fortunately, everything unfolded according to plan, although our journey was far from easy after arriving here.

We lived in constant fear of being discovered as non-citizens. We did our best to blend into society, to blend in unnoticed. My parents displayed remarkable resourcefulness and resilience. Our home was a modest duplex that was covered in graffiti. Nevertheless, we remained grateful for the opportunity to reside in the land of freedom. Therefore, when I finally acquired my own home on my own, for myself and my daughters, it felt like a dream come true. As a little girl, I never would've imagined owning a home in California let alone the United States, especially one just a short stroll away from the breathtaking ocean view. I never would've imagined that I'd be working in the tech industry and especially be given the title, "educator." I wasn't an educator by trade, but life has made me an educator in different ways. That wouldn't have even sounded possible to me, yet here I am. When I arrived at my new home, I decorated the outside with butterflies, butterflies have always symbolized hope for me, and the butterfly decorations made the entire experience even more enchanting, confirming that I was exactly where I was meant to be at precisely the right moment.

Hurt

Just like everyone else, the journey getting here has been full of hurt and struggles, yet it's so easy to feel like nobody understands and that our pains are somehow different than everyone else's. Throughout my life, I've faced adversity and loss and for a while got used to not feeling like I was enough. However, each time life knocked me down, getting up got a little bit easier. Each time I lost, I found a way to win, and every time I've shared, I've realized that I'm not alone. We are all going through something, and it's so important to remember that pain and struggles are just lessons that we must learn to get to the next level, and after we learn them, we have a responsibility to share them with others who need them. This is how I've been able to grow through it all and not allow myself to be stuck in the thick of life.

Since middle school, I constantly compared myself to others from the way I looked to how I felt about my worth. I allowed myself to be defined by the words others told me and allowed those words to cause me to doubt my capabilities. I hated myself. At times, I wanted to disappear. myself. Looking back, I see how all of that comparison and doubt were only noise and distractions that fed my insecurities. Today, I constantly whisper to that little girl that I am enough, and not to compare herself to anyone else because she's incomparable. She's unique and there's no one like her in the entire world because there isn't. Each of us brings something unique, and it's our individuality that makes us special. I was enough but I just didn't see it at the time. There is power in learning how to focus on just ourselves and what we are doing. I learned to water my own grass because it's not greener on the other side. Those people are just watering their own grass.

I was already working at a job without a degree, and I noticed that other people with degrees were getting promoted. I felt embarrassed about not having a degree and every time someone would ask me I would lie or come up with excuses. The issue is that underserved kids, kids like my younger self who don't have parents who can guide them or tell them what they need to do must look outside for guides. For me, it started with seeing others around me getting promoted and wondering what they had that I didn't. I had to put the pieces together. So, it's very important for people that become those kids' guides, that they're very specific in that list because if I knew what I needed to do sooner, I would have done it. To eliminate this barrier, I decided to do what I had to do to check that box off my list. This was me watering my own grass. I enrolled at the University of Phoenix, which is a school for working adults, and simultaneously enrolled in classes at a community college. In six months, I had my bachelor's in science degree in Marketing with an emphasis on marketing. Even though there is a taboo around getting a degree from a prestigious university, I have found that my degree from the University of Phoenix has been just as credible. I have been using it for twenty years, and nobody has ever questioned where I got my degree from. It was a checkmark that resolved the issue for me, and I no longer have to explain myself. I recommend this path to anyone who can't follow the traditional route. Get it done, however you can, to eliminate barriers.

Hope

Once I opened myself up to the world, the world opened up to me. With hope, even just a little, there's an opportunity, and where there's opportunity there's a chance. Hope heals hurt, and if we can learn to focus on hope, we can move past the hurt by continuing to knock on doors, talk to people, and plug away until an opportunity presents itself. I have been working at a top technology company for fifteen years. There are many presentations done in boardrooms and on stages during events. When I would attend those stage events I would be sitting in the front row every time. I asked myself if I could ever be on one of those stages myself. I immediately talked myself out of it. At work, I would offer my time to give tours of the beautiful buildings. The building had a gym, basketball court, and all the amenities you can think of. During one of those tours with a group of youth from nearby farm communities, a young man said to me, "This is nice, but no way someone like me could ever be at a place like this." Little did he know I was just like him, I was not just a tour guide, and for the first time to give someone HOPE I opened up about my humble beginnings. A few months later my humble story was selected and I became a keynote speaker on a stage. I had done it - I was on a stage. A stage I thought wasn't for me. A story I thought was not for the world, but I was wrong. That story has turned into a HOPE story for many. HOPE is fundamental and the first step in the journey of better.

Hustle

Hard work never lies. I've discovered that with all jobs, you just need to know how to work. Whatever it is you're selling, whether it's a service, or a product, learn all the ins and outs of it. Ask questions and give it your all. I think we need to take out the taboo that we need to know every detail of a job to do it because we don't. We just need people to give us a chance, to sit down and get to know us, and to see that we're going to hustle for them. The cool thing about the technology industry is you don't need to know it because it's constantly changing. Every job that I've ever gotten, I didn't know much or anything about. I hustled and put all my effort into learning whatever it was that I was hired to do.

Around the time I obtained my degree, I had the opportunity to choose between two job offers. One was from a mobile company called Handspring, which was a PalmPilot company before the iPhone was introduced. The other offer was from a trade show company that organized events, which appealed to me because I enjoy throwing parties. However, the events company offered a salary that was almost $20,000 higher than the mobile company. At that time, mobile phones were not as popular as they are now, so I was unsure about the mobile industry. However, I had learned from past mistakes of choosing a job solely based on money, so I decided to prioritize the work environment and the people I would be working with. I chose the mobile company because I liked the people and the vibe there and had a personal recommendation from a friend. Despite the lower salary, I believed that if I enjoyed what I do, I would excel at it and have opportunities for growth. And indeed, within a year or two, I was earning a similar amount of money and was happy with my decision. Unfortunately, the company I worked for, Handspring, faced challenges when Apple launched the iPhone, leading to layoffs. Suddenly, I found myself without a job. However, I had built a strong network of connections during my time at the company, and just as my unemployment benefits were running out my former manager Claire, offered me a three-month opportunity at the technology company she worked at. Although I had no experience in software, having worked at a mobile company, I recognized that it's not about what I know. It's about who I knew and how much I was going to hustle. I recognize my hunger for growth and my need to evolve so that I can shatter the glass ceilings that tend to limit people like me. The hustle factor is what will determine your success in whatever you are doing.

Help

One thing is certain in life, there are going to be ups and downs, but if we're going to hurt, which we are, then we might as well make it count. Helping others is how you repurpose your pain and make it count for something. It then becomes the gift that keeps on giving. Once I stopped hiding in the shadows, released the shame of where I came from and started using my voice, I liberated myself from so much unnecessary baggage that I had been carrying with me for most of my life. I also have been able to empower and inspire others to do the same. Feeling like an outsider in the country you live in, everywhere you go, every day, is exhausting. Eventually, it can wear us down and before we know it, we succumb to the belief that everyone has about us. But it doesn't have to be that way. People like me, first-gen American citizens, need to hear more stories like mine. They need to know that they are not alone and to know that it is alright to embrace our individuality and own it. It's alright to use our voice and ask for help and to grow outside the confines of what we know.

Supportive individuals who have faith in you and are willing to vouch for you and provide recommendations are crucial in both personal and professional settings. These are the people who will support you during difficult times and also refer you for opportunities in the workplace. This kind of support is invaluable and can greatly impact your career. While platforms like LinkedIn now serve as a networking tool, the concept of building a strong network of supporters has always been important, because I know I didn't get to where I am alone. It's a result of an accumulation of people who have supported me, referred me, and opened doors for me. As a result, I believe that I have a responsibility to do the same for others. I believe we all do.

Heart

The most beautiful castles sit behind the tallest walls, guarded, and protected from the outside world; some not even visible to anyone on the other side. Perhaps it's necessary, but it's this exact concept and societal norm of guarding and protecting the things we have that are beautiful and rare that isolates us from fully experiencing life. We subconsciously internalize this concept and slowly build walls around our hearts, laying down a brick with each disappointment and heartbreak. Then, before we know it, nobody on the outside can see us. We remain hidden away, nice and safe, behind our walls, all alone. The comfort of the walls eases us into forgetting that the same beauty that we're trying so hard to protect, is the exact divine gift that was meant to be shared so that others could do the same. Our hearts are meant to experience all aspects of life, the sadness, and pain as well as the happiness and love, for one cannot exist without the other. Despite what we may feel at times, our hearts were meant to endure while open and seen because to do this requires us to fully see ourselves. It is through this process that we learn how to love ourselves in all our glory because you have no other choice when you're no longer hiding or running. Stepping out from behind our walls is the bravest thing a person can do, because it's so easy to stay within the comfort of our walls and not allow anyone in. Yet, growth is never comfortable because it requires you to be vulnerable. Building genuine connections with people goes beyond surface-level interactions. It involves getting to know them on a deeper level, even if it's just one level deeper. You do this by having meaningful conversations and showing genuine interest in their lives. This can be done through activities like having lunch together, having Zoom calls, and discussing personal topics like family and interests. By establishing these deeper connections, trust is built, and people are more likely to support and believe in each other. Remember to be yourself when interacting with others in corporate settings or during networking events. Surround yourself with people who appreciate and understand your true self, as they will be the ones who can confidently vouch for you in the future. It's important to bring your whole self to every situation because pretending to be someone else is exhausting and will eventually be discovered. During job interviews or creating relationships through networking, focus on establishing a connection and determining if there is compatibility between you and the company or the person. That job or that relationship needs to be a good fit for you too. It's perfectly acceptable to decline a job offer or not want to network with certain people if you feel that it's not the right fit for you. This is how you continue to keep authentic relationships in your network. These believers, or supporters, play a crucial role in your personal and professional growth. It is important to nourish these relationships by staying connected, sending birthday wishes, checking in on each other, and showing genuine care and interest. Ultimately, friendship is the ultimate networking tool, because it creates strong and lasting connections. Opening up and using your heart to connect with others is how the synergy of people helping one another is activated.

Throughout my journey, I have assumed numerous roles and titles. I have been the daughter, the undocumented citizen, the girl with a different skin color, the mother, the wife and then ex-wife, the friend, the confidant, the author, the speaker, and the business-woman. At times, these titles have defined me and determined my worth. For many years, I struggled to either deny or conform to the expectations that came with each title bestowed upon me. However, the more I tried to fit in, the more disconnected I felt from my true self. Through traveling the various dimensions of my life and witnessing the different versions of myself, I discovered my authentic identity. I came to realize that I was never meant to fit into a single title, especially since my journey began when my mother entrusted me to a coyote to bring me into the United States. This pivotal moment opened my eyes to the fact that I am a girl who embodies experiences and wisdom from two distinct worlds. The common thread that binds these worlds together became apparent when I fully embraced and appreciated my own uniqueness. Embracing my multifaceted nature does not mean forgetting where I come from. Instead, it means finding a way to carry my roots with me wherever I go. I am no longer defined by a title; I am free to simply be myself. In doing so, I am creating opportunities for others to do the same, not only in the realms of technology and business but in life as a whole.

I am part of the three-percent of Latinos in the technology industry. I have been in Sound, Mobile, and Software - I've also cleaned toilets and almost didn't graduate. Believers in me have given me the opportunity to learn, to add value to their companies. If I can give advice to anyone entering any new environment or doing something new - it is to maximize it. Stretch it out as far as it can. Immigrants have been coming to this country for decades - they have maximized their opportunities in this amazing new place so why can't the same be applied to everything? Peace and Love everybody.

SILVIA ELIAT

Co-Founder & Consultant,
Developer Resource Group, LLC

Accomplished and passionate Latina with over 25 years of progressive career experience with a proven record of developing profitable brands. A strategic thinker who has progressed into leadership roles with Fortune 500 Companies in Multicultural Marketing and Finance.

Silvia is also an entrepreneur, a member of WEV (Women's Economic Ventures) IAW (International Association of Women, ANA (Association of National Advertisers), MRM (Multicultural Marketing Resources Inc), and Financial Service Professionals. Silvia is the Northeast Regional President of HLX+ focusing on Latino Thought leadership leveraging key Bridges: Education, Health & Wellness, Culture, Arts & Entertainment, Representation & Gender Equity, Entrepreneurship & Economic Progress.

Take a Chance

In the vibrant city of México City, I was born and raised in a devout Catholic family, where strong moral values and unwavering support surrounded me. As the third of six children, my heart was filled with an insatiable desire to explore the world, carve out a successful career, and uplift my beloved family. While my parents may not have amassed great wealth, acquired properties, or embarked on extravagant travels, their unwavering dedication to our education was their greatest gift. They toiled tirelessly, ensuring that we were equipped with the tools to thrive in life, fostering a future where self-reliance would be our guiding light.

My mother, despite her limited education that halted at junior high school, was a testament to resilience and determination. However, her journey was not without its challenges. My grandfather, a man shaped by traditional beliefs, held the notion that women's sole purpose in life was to marry, care for their husbands, bear children, and tend to household chores. This mindset, rooted in a bygone era, failed to recognize the boundless potential within women.

My mom used to share with us the challenges she faced while growing up, and she was determined to ensure that we didn't experience the same hardships. Despite a back injury she sustained in a severe bus accident when she first met my dad in the early 50's, she never let her health problems hold her back. Over the years, she underwent multiple back surgeries, but her faith, positive attitude, strength, and perseverance allowed her to overcome her fears and limitations. I definitely inherited my mom's "can-do attitude," inner strength, perseverance, and refusal to give up. I became very close to my oldest sister Gloria Luz, because my mom was constantly bedridden or in the hospital when I was just a little girl. It was incredibly difficult for her, not being able to show up the way she wanted to for us while we were still young. However, we were fortunate enough to have a strong family system that supported us and my dad when we needed it the most. My grandmother from my father's side would help take care of us while my father would go to work and provide for the family. Despite the challenges, I have fond memories of my childhood. My siblings and I were close, played together and had a few fights here and there like any other family with six kids. We learned to share and take care of each other.

We were all good students and challenged each other to do better. We all had chores at home and participated in additional school activities. I always liked theater and poetry as well as dancing, while some of my siblings enjoyed martial arts, biking, swimming, playing tennis, etc. My dad worked hard all week long but on weekends he was dedicated to us. We all were looking forward to the weekend to do something fun. My dad also loved outdoor activities since he once was a Boy Scout and used to tell us stories about his hiking adventures with my uncle and his best friend. My sister Gloria Luz and I shared similar interests in music, American football, and boys. I used to ask her questions and advice about dating while I was growing up since she had her first boyfriend at fifteen years old. In those days, I was ashamed to ask my mother those questions. Although my sister was only five years older than me, she became my best friend and confidant. She was my rock, and always found a way to calm me down because growing up I had a rebellious spirit and would often get angry and fired up about things. My sister knew me better than anybody else. She knew my secrets and my strong desire to become a mother one day. I tried several times to get pregnant and after several tests, I found out that I couldn't have kids. She suffered and cried with me when I told her the news. Her nurturing presence and loving manner always inspired me and motivated me to keep going. She used to tell me that I would go on to live a long wonderful and happy life because I had everything to win. I used to constantly ask God why

I couldn't conceive a child and become a mom like every other woman. I used to think that there was something wrong with me or that I had done something wrong to deserve this fate. I felt suffocated, incomplete and a failure as a woman, however, I was not going to allow this situation to define me, so I decided to take care of my mental health and a good friend of mine referred me to a professional. That is one of the best decisions I've made in my life. After three years in therapy, I was finally able to breathe and feel whole as a woman again.

My dad also played a huge role in my life helping me find my passion and purpose in life, and my relationship with him was very strong. He worked as a Creative Director for Ogilvy & Mather Ad Agency in Mexico City, where he achieved numerous awards throughout his career. However, my dad was a go-getter and was always on the lookout for additional opportunities and also worked as a freelancer for other ad agencies. He believed in the mantra of "work hard and play hard." His inner child was always alive, and it helped make the difficulties we faced as a family a bit easier to deal with. I believe that was always the backbone of my foundation growing up, having strong support and a family unit. We all filled in for each other's weak areas, and we made it work.

My siblings and I attended private schools and excelled academically. I felt an obligation to contribute to the financial security of my family. I decided to pursue a career in marketing later in life because I was inspired by my dad working in the Advertising world and felt that it was a perfect fit for me. I liked the idea of creative thinking working with clients and developing campaigns to help them achieve their business goals. Additionally, I had a strong desire to learn languages, particularly English. I quickly absorbed language skills and my parents encouraged me to focus on that passion.

As I began working, I found opportunities to interact with English-speaking individuals, both in my job and in school. I also decided to study French, as I saw the value in being trilingual and believed it would open more job opportunities for me. This drive and determination allowed me to progress in my career and take on different roles within Corporate America. At the age of twenty, I embarked on my professional career. I worked for the beverage Industry Pepsi and Jugos del Valle for nine years. My boss at Pepsi, VP of Sales and Marketing took me under his wing and became my mentor and inspired me in ways that nobody had before. He believed in me and gave me responsibilities that I had never taken on before. He allowed me to shadow him and encouraged me to learn more about the marketing world, always prompting me to ask questions, understand the problem, and find solutions. He also knew about my aspirations to have my own business one day, and he supported me wholeheartedly. He saw the potential in me and told me that I had what it takes to succeed. Even though others were intimidated by him, I never felt that way. We developed a strong friendship. I was quite young at the time, yet I was able to see beyond his title and focus on the person he was. He would push me to take on new challenges and sometimes I would feel overwhelmed. But I never said, "I can't do it". Instead, I would take a step back, think about what he was trying to tell me, and then prepare my questions. I observed how others interacted with him and learned how to manage up, down, and sideways in the organization. In times of feeling overwhelmed, I learned to focus my energy on my "why," always reminding myself why I am doing what I am doing. I've found that answering this simple question really helped me get things done and move on.

After nine years in the beverage industry, I moved to the Hospitality Industry (Hotel Melia and Calinda) for two years and then moved to Televisa, where I had the opportunity to work within the entertainment industry. One of the projects I worked on was the Concurso Señorita México, where Lupita Jones was crowned Miss

Universe (1991). This experience taught me a lot and allowed me to see the importance of quick thinking and being able to work efficiently under pressure.

I developed strong relationships and connections with different Industries, so I decided it was time to be independent and start my own business as an entrepreneur. My PR and Events service agency fulfilled the needs of the companies I worked for earlier. I became the "go to" agency for all of them. Trust and Reliable were among the reasons for them to hire me.

A year after I started my business, I met my husband Alain who is French American and went to Mexico to do business in Exports and Imports and became one of my clients. Alain and I clicked from the beginning and became very good friends over the years before finding each other again at a hotel bar with some friends crying over lost relationships. A year or so later, we moved in together.

Unfortunately, the Mexican peso crisis of 1994 struck, causing widespread economic turmoil and affecting businesses across the country. This crisis marked one of the first international financial crises triggered by capital flight and the unemployment rate sky-rocketed. My entire family lost everything, including me and Alain. As a result, all of us had to move in together and live in a one-bedroom apartment. In the middle of trying to survive that chaotic time, it felt as if everything we had worked for over the years was for nothing. We had lost absolutely everything, yet, what we did have was each other's love and support. Alain and I realized that recovery would take years, prompting us to make the difficult decision to leave the country for the U.S.. We would travel to NJ where Alain's family settled when they migrated to the States from France in the early 60's. This decision plunged me into an emotional roll-ercoaster, torn between not wanting to abandon my family and the need to secure a better future. My sister Gloria Luz who was now living with my parents and pregnant with her second child. I wanted to be there for her just as much as she was there for me when I was growing up. We waited for the baby to be born before leaving Mexico. Leaving felt like the most selfish option as if I was only considering what was best for myself and not my family as a whole. I also realize now, that often when we are making decisions from an already high emotional state, our decisions could be skewed based on emotions rather than assessing the impact in the long run. Sometimes, it takes someone on the outside to give us a more rational viewpoint, and that, combined with faith in God, can often set you on the right path. I know that this was the case for me when I was faced with that difficult decision: should I stay in Mexico with my family or venture into the unknown with my future husband? My sister Gloria Luz didn't stop me, she supported me like she always did and was happy about the opportunity in front of me. She knew I would come back to see them, which I made the promise and always kept it.

The pros and cons of the entire situation were filtered through shame and guilt stemming from my perception that I was abandoning my family. It was a choice that weighed heavily on my heart, and I turned to prayer for guidance. I sought God's help, asking for a sign to show me the right path. Soon after, in a moment of clarity, my now husband spoke words of reassurance and support. He reminded me that I was not alone and that I could only truly help my family if I took care of myself first. With his encouragement, I made the bold decision to accompany him to the United States. Looking back, I see that God speaks to each of us in ways that will understand exactly at the time that we need to hear from him. I only needed to surrender myself to asking for guidance instead of trying to figure it all out myself. As a result, the support that my husband gave me turned out to be what I needed at that time. The challenge was to regain confidence and start from scratch in a place and city that I had never been to before.

In 1995, we left Mexico and embarked on a new chapter of our lives together living with Alain's mother for one year before we were able to afford our place once again. We got married the following year, and in 1998, I landed my first job in a Financial Institution, First Data/Western Union International, a prominent money transfer company in the U.S. Over the years, I climbed the corporate ladder, earning multiple promotions and traveling internationally. Along the way, I had the privilege of meeting incredible people from all walks of life who became my mentors, friends, and family. As I was working and developing my Marketing career in the U.S., I was always in touch with my family. I would call my sister and my parents once a week and send them money monthly. I felt proud of myself for being able to support them financially again.

Right when I thought that everything was fine and we were all moving on with our lives, we found out that my sister Gloria Luz was going to the doctor to check on a lump she felt on her breast. Unfortunately, it was stage four cancer. The devastating news prompted me to travel to Mexico and stay for months at a time to be with her. Her prognosis wasn't good, and her doctor put her on a clinical trial. We all were devastated by the news and were determined to support her and get her whatever she needed to win this battle. My sister and her children son Jonatan were living with my parents, which was a blessing for my sister who started her chemo treatment and needed all the support and care to beat the disease. For seven years, my sister remained positive, never complained, and did everything the doctors told her to do. There were good days and bad days. A year or so before her passing, my two other sisters, Laura, Lupita and I decided to take my sister with us to celebrate New Year at one of the Hotels in Mexico City that were having a dinner dance party. My sister loved to dance! We booked the room with the idea of staying overnight and spending quality time together as sisters. That night we laughed, cried, danced, and talked for hours. My sister Gloria Luz and I were sharing a room and while we were getting ready to go to bed, my sister sat me down and told me something that would change my life forever. She knew she was going to die, and she was worried about her youngest son, who was twelve years old already. Alain and I were his Godparents and were very close to him. My sister hugged me and said: I need you to take care of Jonatan when I'm gone. This is my gift to you, take care of him, you wanted to be a mother, and he is now your son! I know you and Alain will be excellent parents. We cried all night and I promised we would take care of him as our son. My sister lost her battle with breast cancer eleven years ago, and it felt like a piece of my heart went with her when she left. Yet, the last thing she did for me was to grant me my wish to become a mother when she asked me to adopt my nephew her child after her passing. My sister gave me my life back and my WHY became stronger and clearer than ever. It took us 3 years to be able to bring Jonatan to the States. It was a difficult and grueling process, but we were determined to bring him home.

Throughout this journey, I have discovered my strength and resilience. I have realized that my words have power, my presence is meaningful, and my culture and heritage hold great significance. I am a woman with moral values and dreams, just like anyone else. And now, I am determined to share my story and inspire others to move forward and believe in themselves. My life is my legacy. My "Why" is what moves and drives me to move forward and pushes me every day to learn new things and to believe in the power of love, family, and community. I want my grandchildren and the next generation to know that we have paved the way for them to be successful, but they have to do their part and work hard. Dream big, don't take things for granted, be humble and have a grateful heart, take a chance, and don't fear the unknown because at the end of the day, everything is going to be okay. You are not alone!

CARLOS QUEZADA

VP of Customer Experience
and Digital Engagement Strategy

Carlos Quezada, a trailblazing Latino executive, currently serves as the Vice President of Customer Experience and Digital Engagement for a leading global Fortune 100 tech company. With an impressive 25-year career in the tech industry, Carlos has defied norms and earned recognition as one of the top 100 most influential Latinos in tech for three consecutive years. Hailing from Degollado, Jalisco, Mexico, Carlos immigrated to the U.S. at 14, embarking on an unconventional journey to reach the pinnacle of corporate success. Driven by gratitude, he sees it as his purpose to empower fellow Latinos and immigrants, actively engaging in community initiatives to inspire, educate, and foster success.

The Roadmap to Success

Earlier this year, I was taken aback by the overcoming sense of astonishment, while sitting on a plane back home from a company meeting in Texas. It was a meeting that I wasn't invited to, but I decided to show up anyway. As I gazed out the window, I was greeted by the breathtaking sight of the sun rising over the vast empty land. The warm rays of sunlight illuminated the plane, casting a golden glow on everything it touched. At that moment, I couldn't help but reflect on how far I've come in my career. It's so easy to get lost in the next item on our to-do list that we forget to celebrate the victories and small wins. I know I do. Yet, it's important, and this particular trip was definitely a win not just for me, but for my team.

Despite all my accomplishments and advancements, there's always a lingering feeling that there is still so much more to do. It's not just about my own professional growth, but also about helping others who come from similar circumstances and are striving to elevate their lives from nothing. I recognized the unique struggles that my people face in navigating the big tech world as a minority. In our communities and families, there aren't many mentors or tangible success stories to guide us.

Looking back, I realized that ten years ago, I would never have had the confidence to fly to a meeting I wasn't invited to. I always felt like I didn't belong in those rooms because of where I come from and the college I didn't graduate from (I only attended a trade school). It took a lot of time, coaching, and experience to cultivate confidence within myself. The sneaky impostor syndrome is what I describe as a monster never truly goes away, but with every intentional bold action, it takes a backseat in my mind.

Entering that meeting uninvited was the boldest move I had ever made, and surprisingly, it ended up working in my favor. I work for a company that is part of a larger, more established company. There was always this underlying sense that the key decisions were being made by the parent company, and we had to absorb those decisions. This bothered me because I believed that our company perspective was more innovative and ahead of the curve. Adopting the mindset of a larger company seemed counterproductive to me.

I realized that I couldn't just accept this situation. I had to find a way to communicate to the rest of the company, from the "mothership," that we actually had a head start on the work being developed. To do this, I had to elevate and showcase the work that my team was doing. I also had to build strong partnerships and ally ships across the company to help elevate and sponsor our work.

This led to an opportunity for me to present in front of the CEO uninvited. It was a risky move that could have potentially cost me my job. However, I felt confident because of the strong partnerships and relationships I had built prior to the meeting. I knew I had enough sponsors in the room who would support and guide the conversation. This experience reinforced the importance of building strong partnerships. It showed me that by taking bold actions and cultivating meaningful relationships, I can overcome any obstacle and make a significant impact in my career and the lives of others.

So, the morning of, I gathered up my courage and faith, crossed myself since I am Catholic, and as I walked into the building, I felt a mix of nerves and determination. The door to the meeting room seemed larger than life, towering over me. As I approached, I noticed a woman stationed at a table with pre-printed badges. Remembering the importance of confidence, I approached her with a sense of purpose, holding my coffee in one hand and my backpack slung over one shoulder. I asked her about the meeting, pretending to search for my badge among the others on the table, even though I knew I wasn't supposed to be there. My act seemed to confuse her, and she quickly apologized for the oversight. She handed me a sticky note and asked me to write my name and title so she could print a badge for me. I still have that sticky note as a reminder of that moment.

With my makeshift badge in hand, she opened the door for me, and I stepped into the conference room. Instantly, I spotted my sponsors, the people I had built strong relationships with. Seeing their familiar faces put me at ease in this unfamiliar space. They had no idea I wasn't officially invited, and I used that to my advantage, attaching myself to them and pretending like I belonged. They became my networking anchors, providing a sense of familiarity and support.

There were a few individuals in the room who knew why I was there and applauded my boldness. Their recognition and encouragement further boosted my confidence. They took it upon themselves to inform others about my presence and purpose. By the time it was my turn to present, the room was aware of my intentions and ready to listen.

They also contributed to the charade of Carlos being supposed to be there, seamlessly blending in with the situation. When I finally got the opportunity to present, it went very smoothly because so many people were in on it and supportive. The CEO had no idea it was never on the agenda.

The meeting was amazing, and as a result of my presentation, I was asked to take on two highly visible initiatives for the company. I had to fly back to this meeting every month to give updates on the progress. At that point, my team and I had a seat at the table. I was given the opportunity to speak during a two-day workshop. There was a thirty-minute slot in the agenda that was related to my team's work, and I stepped in to present instead of the originally scheduled person. I had rallied enough support on day one, and they updated the agenda for day two to include my name as the speaker for that slot.

Since then, we have been participating at a very senior level with this company and driving its transformation. That moment really springboarded my career, and in January, I was promoted to vice president of that function. I was brought over to the larger organization to continue what I was doing but with a broader reach across the entire company. My team has grown by about 200% since then, and we now have a global presence. Along with my promotion to vice president I also had the opportunity to elevate the rest of my team within the company. One expression that I often say is, "It's only lonely at the top if you don't bring others with you." Helping others reach the top is just as rewarding to me.

I want to lead by example and make real connections that have a lasting impact on the lives of people around me because that is the true essence of sustainability in what we do. The only way to do that is by showing up being yourself, being vulnerable as a leader, and connecting with others from that place. The key to our success lies in our ability to not take ourselves too seriously and simply enjoy the journey. That's the mindset of every team that I've led, and I see it throughout my entire team. Every time I engage with somebody, people genuinely enjoy working with our team. They're having fun, they feel like they can trust us. There are no egos, and it's beautiful to see.

The more I tell my story, the more I realize that it's not that different from other people's stories. Many of us have stories of survivalism and grit. What sets us apart is how we leverage those experiences to learn and grow. While everyone's staircase to success may look different, the desires of each of us are the same. We all want better for our children and to break the generational curses of our bloodline. However, wanting and knowing how to achieve these things are very different. I have yet to meet a person who doesn't want a better life. The issue is that many people are unaware of how to get to where they want to be.

I've learned that the first step to giving our children a different life and breaking generational curses is to not project our fears onto them. We can do this by continuing to broaden our own horizons so that we're exposed to different experiences. As a result, our children will also be exposed to different things, which will broaden their horizons too. We all stand on our parents' shoulders, and while some may have built more for us to stand on than others, that is our starting point and what we have to work with. Keeping that in mind, we should seek to learn how to stand taller by building more for ourselves which our children will stand on.

I remember growing up and cleaning offices and banks with my mother after school. I always felt like I was in the behind-the-scenes moments, never getting to see the offices with people in them. I used to wonder what meetings took place in the conference rooms that we cleaned, what business was conducted in them; what big life-changing decisions were conducted right there in the very room we were cleaning up after. I never got to know the answers to those things as a child, but now, during the summer vacation, my son comes to the office to work with me every day. I don't want him to wonder what it looks like when people are here. He sits in meetings with me, and he's not intimidated by the shiny, big office building. I would have been terrified of that at his age, but he has no problem. He even joined a video conference I had with the CEO of the company. As a child his age, I would have been terrified to walk into a conference room with thousands of people and raise my hand to ask a question, but he's done that and it's something that I love. Although I know he will grow up with fears of his own because we all do, I refuse to pass my fears on to him. I want to break those generational cycles and recognize that the fears instilled in us die with us.

Throughout my journey, I have encountered numerous obstacles that I have had to overcome. These challenges have pushed me to confront my own fears and step out of my comfort zone. I have come to understand the significance of forming strong partnerships, taking courageous actions, and being unafraid to assert myself even when not explicitly invited. By embracing these principles, I have been able to elevate my career and bring others along on this journey of growth and achievement.

However, it is important to note that my journey is not solely focused on personal success. It is also about making a lasting impact and helping others achieve their own goals. I know that every door that I'm able to open for someone else is another opportunity to make a real lasting impact in this world, and not just through that one person's life but their family's as well. It only takes one person in a family to step up to the occasion of life and do something different, striving for more to steer the entire bloodline in a different, higher direction. I believe in the power of collaboration and supporting others in their endeavors because it is only through this manner that each and every one of us has been able to achieve our dream regardless of where we're from or what color skin we have. We all are where we are because someone helped us along the way. By lifting others up, and providing guidance and assistance, I can contribute to a collective sense of achievement and fulfillment.

The immigrant journey can be compared to a winding river, with each milestone representing a bend in the current towards success. The first bend, known as 'Gen zero,' symbolizes the parents' initial arrival in the new country. From there, every achievement, such as finding employment, mastering English, or graduating from high school, becomes a current that propels the entire family forward.

As the next generation enters the scene, they join the river from a higher point, benefiting from the steady flow created by their parents. They can then navigate this river to achieve even greater success in various aspects of their lives, including financial stability, career advancements, and social integration.

However, it's important to acknowledge that obstacles can arise along the way. The next generation may encounter rapids that hinder their progress. For instance, if they choose not to pursue higher education, they might find it more challenging to navigate the currents towards well-paying jobs. Involvement in negative influences or dropping out of high school can also create turbulent waters on their journey toward success.

To navigate this river effectively, it's crucial to assess our current position and identify areas for improvement. By understanding the flow of the river, we can make informed decisions and take actions that steer us toward success. This concept is often discussed in workshops, where we encourage participants to visualize their own immigrant journey and develop strategies to navigate the river smoothly without getting swept away.

Molding is often seen as a form of control, but I believe it is more about shaping a person's core values. These core values serve as the foundation for their decision-making process. Exposure plays a crucial role in building this foundation and molding these values. In my family, it would have been acceptable and normal if I grew up being a construction worker. Nobody in my family would have looked down on that in my family because the expectation was just me having a job. Now, as I bring my son into this current environment that I work in, I can see that he understands this as the norm- an office, a nice building, working with educated people. He may choose to work in an office or even in a futuristic setting like a spaceship, but at the very least, he understands that where I'm at is the normal, the standard expectation, and he knows that hard work and dedication are essential.

By molding our children's values, we are providing them with a solid floor to stand on. This floor represents the minimum expectations we have for them, such as a strong work ethic and a commitment to personal growth. From this foundation, they can then build their own unique path and make their own decisions. Molding is not about controlling their every move, but rather about instilling in them the values and principles that will guide them towards success and fulfillment.

It is important to recognize that your current position may often be someone else's aspiration. While you may not perceive yourself as successful, some individuals would love to be in your shoes. This realization should inspire you to help others who are still striving to reach the level you have achieved. By offering guidance and support, you can make a positive impact on their journey.

Furthermore, it is crucial to always be in a state of growth and expansion. Settling for where you are can hinder your progress and limit your potential. At the same time, you must always be in a state of gratitude for where you are at, because it is only through the culmination of your experiences that you are here, and gratitude is truly the key to happiness regardless of what else is going on around you. However, to continue moving forward, you must constantly seek new opportunities and challenges, and by doing this you strengthen your resourceful nature as well as your abilities. This could involve acquiring new skills, pursuing further education, or exploring different areas of interest. Embracing a mindset of continuous improvement will ensure that you never become complacent and that you are always striving for personal and professional growth, pushing your family further and further down the river, and putting yourself in a position to be able to open more doors for others.

In order to determine your next steps, it is helpful to set goals and create a roadmap for your future. Where would you like to be in three months, six months, and one year? What would you like to be doing? What is one of the most important goals that you'd like to accomplish? Identify areas where you want to develop and outline the necessary actions to achieve those goals, breaking the larger goals up into bite-size, manageable steps. This could involve seeking out mentors or role models who can provide guidance, networking with professionals in your desired field, or taking on new projects or responsibilities. By asking yourself the correct questions you gain clarity on where to actively seek out opportunities for growth so that you can push yourself outside of your comfort zone. This is how you can avoid complacency and continue to progress toward your next level of success. Remember, growth is a lifelong journey, and it requires constant effort and determination, but it will always be up to you to keep moving forward. When life gets difficult, and it will because that's what it does at times, you must learn how to find ways to keep the momentum, to sustain the motivation, even if you must borrow it from elsewhere. Whatever works for you is what you have to learn to implement into your daily rituals, and I promise you, the older version of yourself will be grateful you did.

ENTREPRENEURSHIP, ECONOMIC PROGRESS & FINANCE

MARK MADRID

United States Army Honorary Colonel

A first-generation high-school and college graduate, the Honorable Mark Leroy Madrid is a product of education, unrelenting grit, signature energy, and fanatic discipline. From a farming community to Wall Street to nonprofit to government, he dedicates his life to economic empowerment for all. Mark has been recognized by both his alma maters. He was awarded the Community Emerging Legacy Award by the University of Texas at Austin Division of Diversity and Community Engagement. The University of Notre Dame Mendoza College of Business named Mark the recipient of Mendoza's Alumni Service Award. Mark is Honorary Colonel for the U.S. Army.

FAITH, DISCIPLINE, ENERGY, VICTORY, AND LEROY

From a farming community to Wall Street to fulfillment

"Faith is the substance of things hoped for, the evidence of things not seen." "Live energetically with faith and believe in yourself."

God is super great, and I am living a dream, although it took overcoming tragedies and injustices to arrive at this victorious conclusion. I grew up in a Texas Panhandle farming community, known as the cheeseburger capital of Texas. Friona is a special place, revered for small-town values, integrity, and all seasons, from the hottest summers to tornadoes to blizzards. How did I end up there? My father Marcos and mother Maria met in the area as migrant farm workers in the cotton fields. As American citizens, they took on jobs hoeing cotton because that is where the jobs were. Perpetually, I admire the ganas and determination of my parents. They built a welding business from the ground up, with my father's strong hands and my mother's loyalty and resilience. Being raised in a family-owned small business has shaped me and influenced how I lead nationally in support of economic prosperity for all. It is truly an honor to lead, and it gives me unrelenting energy and purpose, while never forgetting where I come from.

I am the youngest of three siblings, with a significant age gap between my sisters and me. My mother always prioritized her children and took great care in dressing us nicely and keeping us meticulously groomed and clean. Even from an early age, I had a fondness for dressing well, and she would dress me up in three-piece suits. Unfortunately, my brother, Leroy, after whom I am named, passed away in a tragic freak accident the year before I was born. He was only five years old. People often ask me where I get my signature and distinguished energy from, and I always say that I am living not just for myself but also for my brother. His memory and the lessons that I learned from his loss shape who I am today. The same is true for my two sisters, Mary Felix, and Dianna Lee Madrid. The accident occurred when Leroy and Dianna were playing with a friend under a flower box suspended by chains with heavy pottery. The chains snapped, causing the flower box to collapse, tragically killing my brother instantly. It is a story that I reflect on every day, as it has profoundly impacted my life. My brother's birthday was around Christmas, and I was born a year after his death. It was not until my thirties that I realized the significance of being born so soon after his passing. Growing up, I struggled during Christmas, feeling like our Christmas tree and gifts were not as prominent as everyone else's. Reflecting on this as an adult, it makes sense. I am sure the holidays were always a devasting time for my parents, but as a child I did not comprehend this.

In 2020, my father passed away from COVID, which has made sharing my story even more critical. Dad, Marcos Madrid, Jr., was not only a pillar of support for our entire family but also for the entire community. If someone's car broke down, the call would come to Marcos. If a family funeral needed a fundraiser, the call would come to Marcos. Unconditionally, he was always there to help solve problems and lend a helping hand. I could reach out to him at any time, and he would answer the phone and talk to me, even when he was on his deathbed. My dad was distinguished in drive, resourcefulness, and energy. My dad and mom launched a welding business in our community, despite not having formal business training. If you drive through the Texas Panhandle or the Texas South Plains, you will see structures that may erode in metal but will remain strong and withstand the test of time. As a child, I would look up at the grain elevator and spot a small figure at the very top, and I knew it was dad, always leading by example and always solving problems. My family bootstrapped with ganas to success. We had humble beginnings and worked hard to get where we are today. We take nothing for granted.

I illustrate my small-town values every day. These values include living with integrity. Although, mutual respect for all did not reside in all. I remember a specific incident when my mother and I were on our way to visit my dad, and she had this beautiful scarf that blew away in the fierce winds of the Texas Panhandle. We went to the high-end store in town to get another one. The family business was prospering. Unexpectedly, my mother was accused of stealing something and was arrested right in front of me. I was only six years old at the time, and I was devastated. I kept telling them that they had no idea who we were and that we had the means to shop there and that we belonged. It was a deeply traumatic experience for me to witness my mother being handcuffed for no reason other than her being a Latina. It was a clear case of marginalization. Thankfully, the situation was eventually resolved, but it left a timeless impact on me. Despite the injustice, my mother showed incredible grace, composure, and strength, and we managed to get through it. However, I will never forget that incident, which drives me every day to advance opportunities for all.

"We hold these truths to be self-evident, that all men are created equal, that they are endowed by their Creator with certain unalienable rights, that among these are Life, Liberty and the Pursuit of happiness."
— Declaration of Independence

I am a proud fourth-generation Mexican American built by ganas. Both of my parents' education went as far as the eighth grade. Although I did not grow up in an academic household, I was rooted in determination. Definitely, ganas was our family trademark. From an early age, I knew instinctively that education would be my pathway to success. Despite growing up in a small farming community with more cattle than people and only one stoplight, I was eager to excel and dream big. I became the first Latinx valedictorian in the town's history, both in eighth grade and high school. This achievement opened the door for a full scholarship at the University of Texas at Austin McCombs School of Business, which catalyzed my way to Wall Street upon graduation. Subsequently, I earned my master's from the University of Notre Dame Mendoza College of Business. No one can ever take your education from you.

Along the journey, I realized that I cultivated discipline, energy, competitiveness, and the will to win from an early age. I recall a transformative moment in second grade in art class. I joined a competition called picture memory, in which a piece of art would be revealed, and students had to identify the artwork and artist. I won first place in the competition, even though art was my least favorite subject. In third grade, I participated in the county spelling bee and faced tough competition. I emerged as the winner. I repeated this victory in fourth grade, as well. I attribute my success to hard work and dedication, as I did not have prior knowledge or context for many of the words. I simply practiced relentlessly with fanatic discipline (thank you, Roxanne Spillett). Notably, I did not see kids that looked like me on those stages, not at that time. I did suffer from racism and marginalism in my hometown, which was painful and destructive. Yet, I was also influenced by some of the greatest humans I'll ever come across. Truly, it was a living paradox, which continued during college and Wall Street.

Notwithstanding, my competitive fire continued with that fanatic energy and discipline, grounded in faith (thank you, Oshea). During my freshman year at the University of Texas at Austin, I was in search of summer work and came across a recruiting flyer from Southwestern Family of Companies promoting a summer internship for ambitious individuals. Being bold and ambitious, I was immediately compelled. Certainly, the recruiters did understate what they meant by ambitious. The job turned out to be selling books door-to-door, and it was an unforgettable, ultra-challenging, and ultimately rewarding leadership experience. Starting out was not easy, as I did not have cash on hand, as others did. I had to collect deposits to purchase inventory, and many students who started this job quit within the first or second week. Fortunately, I managed to survive the summer and received a tough-minded business award for my efforts. Near and dear to my heart, I hold the lifetime lessons of that summer. The internship required completion of a "sales school" in Nashville, Tennessee, followed by randomly selecting a U.S. location to sell books door-to-door. I chose Olathe, Kansas. I had never been to Olathe or Kansas! Since I did not have the money to rent an apartment, I ended up convincing the Kansas State School for the Deaf to offer me subsidized housing for the summer. As taught in sales school, every morning, I would go to the same breakfast diner and after breakfast sing the "bookman/bookwoman" song in the parking lot. The lyrics: "It's a great day to be a bookman, it's the best thing that I know. It's a great day to be a bookman, everywhere I go-o-o. Goodbye no and never, never goodbye doubt and fear. It's a great day to be a bookman and to be of good cheer. Hey!" Locals would see me there every day, at the exact same time, without fail, rain or shine, with discipline and energy. This is when I cultivated relationship building as a core differentiating skill. Eventually the diner patrons that initially befuddled by me became amazingly loyal friends. By the end of the summer, we were attending Kansas City Royals baseball games (their treat).

This summer job proved to serve a bigger purpose in my life than I realized at the time. It served as an everlasting milestone moment of inspiration and resilience that opened unimaginable doors. As a child, my big dream was to make it all the way to New York City. To me, no place was bigger and grander than New York City. Before graduating with honors from the University of Texas at Austin with my accounting degree, I set my tunnel vision on Wall Street. Despite not knowing where to start and not having a mentor, I navigated my way through all the rigorous interviews and eventually landed the position. I had no idea about the sheer intensity of the interview process. It involved nine interviews, both solo and group, lasting about forty-five minutes each. What I did not realize is that even one dissenting view from the nine interviews would disqualify you from consideration. It was grueling, but one theme was recurring in every interview. "So, tell me about the time that you sold books door-to-door in college." I told the story over and over, and I am convinced that the bookman story was a prioritized compensating factor that helped me land that coveted position on Wall Street.

Hebrews 1:11 in the Bible cites, "Faith is the substance of things hoped for, the evidence of things not seen." This verse resonates with me because it reminds me of the importance of having faith in God first leading to faith in oneself. This faith will guide you through troubled waters.

I will never forget a particular incident on Wall Street when I was working on a rigorous project. One of my managers said to me, "Madrid, if you don't get your stuff together, we're going to rip you a new one." Another remarked, "I don't know what it is about you Hispanics; I feel like I have to hold your hands." These statements were shocking and inappropriate even in the mid-nineties. I felt a strong urge to crawl into a hole because being on Wall Street was already intense enough. I was not sleeping much, only three or four hours a night, and my eyes were bloodshot from the long hours and the intensity. But I reminded myself of the saying, "If you can make it there, you can make it anywhere." "We are what we repeatedly do. Excellence, then, is not an act but a habit." Sigue adelante (keep going)!

I subscribe to the Biblical scriptures of faith. During times of uncertainty or when faced with unexpected challenges, I rely on my faith in God. And this faith guided me in overcoming the marginalism on the Street. Subsequently, I prospered on Wall Street, and I have God and family to thank. Also, I thank Dina Pruzansky and Sheryl Heffernan for believing in me. This mindset of sheer faith, discipline, and grit has fueled my determination, regardless of the circumstances. I believe in embracing each day, knowing that tomorrow is a new opportunity, and the sun will always rise. That is why I love the mornings and why I am an early rise or "early bird." My father instilled this habit in me, and it is a way of life for me. I am an Honorary Colonel for the United States Army, and I am reminded that we do more by 9 A.M.. than most people do all day. My designation as Honorary Colonel in itself is an unbelievable story.

It was during my successful banking career that I was on the verge of realizing a childhood dream, becoming a bank president. However, the Great Recession had something else in mind. I will never forget New Year's Eve 2008. "We are shuttering. At this time, do not share with your teams." It was a jolting turn of events that I did not anticipate after all that I had accomplished previously, including on Wall Street. I found myself in a position of starting over, but this time would be notably different. This time, I would lean fully into my Mark Madrid signature hallmarks of faith, discipline, and energy. This is when I pivoted to the Houston Hispanic Chamber of Commerce, where I started at entry level, selling small business memberships, sharing an office cubicle, and managed by someone much younger than me (love you, Manny!). It was a humbling experience, but I was invigorated beyond measure supporting Latina and Latino small businesses. This experience was truly a lightning rod experience. My perpetual gratitude to the Houston Hispanic Chamber of Commerce and President and CEO Dr. Laura Murillo. Eventually, I became the first C-suite executive other than the CEO or the organization. A couple of years into my role, my boss approached me during Hispanic Heritage Month and asked me to address Army soldiers. I was thrilled because of my enduring respect for veterans and those serving in the military. However, I was abundantly anxious about addressing hundreds of soldiers. I remember feeling overwhelmed when I found out that I had to speak for forty-five minutes instead of the expected five minutes. I went to the bathroom in a moment of panic, but I quickly gathered myself and decided to focus on telling undeniably compelling stories about successful Latino and Latina entrepreneurs. What better way to exude Hispanic Heritage? As I waited to take the stage, I calmed my nerves by tapping one of my cowboy boots. This is how I ground myself during stressful times, and it works. I persevered through the presentation, and the Major General praised it as one of the best they had ever seen. Throughout the years, I continued to work with the group. I received a surprise in the mail, the designation as an Honorary Colonel, which resides on a special place on my office wall alongside other milestones, the Jefferson Award and Latino Leaders Maestros Award.

My life is grounded in my faith, discipline, energy, and now victory. Along the way, I have leaned into the power of preparation, as I served as CEO of the Greater Austin Hispanic Chamber of Commerce and CEO of the Stanford Latino Entrepreneurship Initiative / Latino Business Action Network (thank you to the alumni of the scaling program, mi familia por vida).

As Oprah said, "I believe luck is preparation meeting opportunity. If you hadn't been prepared when the opportunity came along, you wouldn't have been 'lucky'." We all know what our best is, and it is important to listen to our inner voice and strive to deliver our best. The more prepared we are, the better equipped we heighten the golden opportunity to deliver our best selves.

Coach Vince Lombardi once said, "I firmly believe that any man's greatest fulfillment is that moment when he has worked his heart out in a good cause and lies exhausted on the field of battle, victorious." This quote has resonated with me and has become the thread of my legacy. I do not view the battle as something negative, but rather as a good battlefield. If I can lay on that field, knowing that I have given my all, then I consider myself victorious. In the past, I may have questioned myself, conceded to imposter syndrome, and self-destructed. Today, I am fully convinced that with the grace of God, I am victorious. This sense of victory fills me with purpose, and I am grateful that I can say that I have lived every ounce of life to its fullest for me and my big brother, Leroy.

Thank you, Mom, Dad, Mary, Dianna, Dan, Neely, Amy, Champ and inner circle friends and family and—most importantly—thank you, God.

Victorious!

STACI LATOISON

Founder & CEO,
Dream Big Ventures

Staci is a venture capitalist, investor, and leader in business strategy and innovation. A 22-year veteran of Chevron, Staci worked to shape and influence energy transition while fueling her passion for empowering others. After leaving Chevron in 2022, Staci established Dream Big Ventures, focusing on investments in the energy and health sectors, and supporting under-represented entrepreneurs. A proud Latina of Puerto Rican and Cuban descent, Staci uses this platform to share her story and motivate others — in particular women, Latinos, and other underestimated groups — to stand confidently in their power, dream bigger, and fearlessly forge their own unique paths.

Dare To Dream Bigger

Single mother. Entrepreneur. Consultant.
Investor. Board member. Paid speaker.

These are some of the "labels" or words that describe me, but I describe myself as a proud Latina mother of Puerto Rican and Cuban descent who has successfully climbed the corporate ladder and is raising two incredible kids (DJ and Sofia). Gratefully, today I am dedicated and, in a position, to empower others, especially women. I can walk into a room with my head held high because of the work I've put into my life and career. I am driven and self-motivated. Yet, I did not always feel this way about myself, and it was those times that molded me to be who I am today.

Let's start from the beginning. As a teenager, being a single mother was the furthest thing on my mind. I witnessed my sister, who is nine years older than me, get pregnant at sixteen and seventeen years old with my nephews, so pregnancy was not part of my plan at all.

My parents married at nineteen and twenty years old; my mom never graduated from high school, and my father served in the Air Force. Since they did not go to college, they instilled in us the importance of getting a college education. However, when my sister got pregnant as a teen, their expectations for me to succeed were even greater, and I had no intention of letting them down. I was a straight-A student and star athlete, was in the National Honor Society, and a varsity basketball standout named to the Texas All-State team in high school, but sometimes our decisions take us down an entirely different path in life than the one we planned.

At seventeen-years-old, I got pregnant with my son. I will never forget the disappointment and shock written all over my parents' faces. They couldn't believe it. They thought I would've learned after seeing the hardships my sister dealt with as a teen mom. At the same time, my parents' mailbox was filling up daily with scholarship offers to Division I colleges around the nation such as West Point, Baylor, Texas Christian University, Southern Methodist University, University of Houston, University of Kentucky, Pepperdine, University of Texas in El Paso, and countless others. I cannot describe how painful it was for me to open them, with tears running down my face and my son kicking in my stomach. I felt like I had let everyone down – my parents, my teammates, my coaches, and myself. Within a few months, I went from being confident in the clear vision I had for my future to feeling like a failure. I was ashamed, scared, and completely confused. I didn't know what I was going to do. To top it off, my parents were so upset with me that they barely spoke to me throughout my entire pregnancy. As disappointed as they felt they were still right by my side in the labor room to witness their grandson enter the world.

Pregnant and with my parents not speaking to me, I decided it was best to move in with my son's father. He was eight years older than I was, which should have been a warning sign that it was wrong to even be in a relationship with him in the first place. Unfortunately, like many other red flags I experienced with him, I justified it.

The verbal and physical abuse began after I gave birth to my son. He beat me up several times throughout our relationship. At one point, I remember feeling so embarrassed and ashamed that I isolated myself from my family because I didn't want to tell anyone what was happening. The young girl with the big hopes and dreams seemed so far from who I had become. I was extremely disappointed in myself and felt detached from who I thought I was. I always said I'd never let anyone hit me and didn't understand how I got to a place of justifying the abuse so quickly. I told myself that my son needed his father around and I didn't want to be the mother who took her son away from his dad. *I learned that it's the excuses we tell ourselves that stand in the way of moving forward to receive our blessings.*

Even as a young girl, I knew deep down that I wanted to be independent. I never wanted to depend on a man or feel stuck in a toxic marriage or unhealthy relationship. Despite these early challenges, I always knew that getting a college degree would afford me better opportunities. A degree would enable me to support my child and succeed beyond my family's history, despite my teenage pregnancy. Therefore, I made a decision: this cycle would stop with me, and I enrolled at the University of Houston.

Before my son's first birthday, I was waiting tables at Pappadeaux Seafood Kitchen to afford diapers and pay my car note, insurance, gas, and daycare. During my sophomore year at the University of Houston, I received a full scholarship from the Gates Millennium Scholars Program via the Hispanic Heritage Foundation. My mom took care of my son while I worked and went to school at night, and I'd pick him up from her house afterward. That was our life in the beginning.

About a year later, I got another job at a State Farm Insurance Agency, after a dire warning from Abuela who had a dream that someone followed me home after my night shift at the restaurant. I always knew I wasn't going to stay with my son's father but was trying to hold off leaving until after I graduated because of a lack of confidence in my ability to provide for my son on my own. A friend of mine who knew about the abuse asked me why I was still with him. That question planted a seed in my mind that pushed me to question myself. Shortly after that, when my son was around two, I decided I couldn't take it anymore. With nowhere else to turn, I had to tell my parents. I don't know where I would be if I had stayed, possibly dead or in prison. *Abuse only escalates. It never gets better.*

My parents let me come back home with my son, and we lived there for a while until I got a place of my own. I got a restraining order and later a protective order against my son's father, and picked up a second job working at night, doing everything in my power to close that chapter in my life and start over.

I believe the Universe supports you when you have faith in yourself. Around that time, a new opportunity opened up for me. A friend told me about his mom, who had him at a young age but still managed to achieve great success at Texaco (now Chevron Corporation). She helped me secure an interview for a cybersecurity internship, which only required good grades. Despite my lack of knowledge in cybersecurity at the age of twenty, I had confidence in my work ethic and desire to learn. This internship turned into a twenty-two-year career with Chevron, allowing me to grow and expand.

I worked my way up the corporate ladder, securing funding and managing multibillion-dollar budgets for international projects which led to unique opportunities to see the world. Was it easy to achieve? Absolutely not. It required a lot of grit, effort, and patience. It took time to prove my abilities. It's not easy to be a Latina, single mother who started her career as an intern in the male-dominated oil and gas industry. I was a minority in my field, and there were many barriers that I had to break to get ahead. *I have seen and felt situations firsthand where you're overlooked because you're a woman. Many times, even if you are more than qualified, as women, we don't rise within a corporation at the same pace that white males do. Therefore, time as well as the ability to speak up for ourselves and ask questions are the currencies to success. However, first, you have to know what questions to ask.*

I have always wanted to travel. As a little girl, I'd often daydream about all the different countries and what it would be like to experience their cultures. As an adult and single mother, I knew that it was only through vigorously pursuing my education and building my career that I would be able to accomplish my goals. As soon as I finished my undergraduate degree, I immediately got my MBA in International Business at the University of St. Thomas in Houston, Texas. I may not have known how it would happen, but deep in my soul, I knew I would eventually fulfill my dreams of traveling.

At a Career Expo held at Chevron, I had a life-changing moment when a fellow Chevron colleague shared her expatriate assignment in Thailand. This was the first time I had heard someone at Chevron talk about overseas opportunities, and it sparked a desire within me to pursue such opportunities. Hearing a woman talk about taking on a global assignment further fueled my wish to move beyond the United States. She inspired me and gave me the confidence to challenge myself. I began asking questions and researching what steps I needed to take to be assigned overseas. It took seven years, but when my son turned ten, I was offered an expatriate assignment in China. It turned out to be one of the most amazing experiences of my life.

At first, it felt surreal that I was raising my son in a foreign country while pursuing my career. It was an amazing adventure that lasted five years — two years in Chengdu and three years in Qingdao. My son mastered Mandarin at the International school he attended, and we traveled all over Southeast Asia. We vacationed in Thailand, Vietnam, Japan, Hong Kong, Macau, Malaysia, Bali, Australia, New Zealand, South Korea, Singapore, and the Philippines. It was an incredibly enriching experience for both of us. Every day, every country felt like a playground. I never in my lifetime thought I'd even get a chance to visit China, let alone live there. This experience not only expanded our perspectives on life but also planted seeds of possibilities for the rest of my family. I sent plane tickets for my parents and my three nephews to visit us multiple times and took them to explore various parts of Asia. Throughout our years in China, we visited the United States once a year during Christmas. The rest of the time, we were completely immersed in our new lives in China.

At thirty-two, life delivered an unexpected yet extraordinary surprise – I was pregnant again. I still vividly recall breaking the news to my fourteen-year-old son in a taxi, asking how he felt about becoming a big brother. His initial shock quickly turned to overjoyed excitement. However, the baby's father, living in Sydney, Australia, had a disheartening opposite reaction to the pregnancy, saying he would not be around if I went through with having the baby. I ignored his cowardice threats and stood firm in my decision. Having successfully raised my son single-handedly from a young age, I was confident in my ability to do it all over again, now with more experience and stability in my life. So, I did. My daughter, born in Beijing, China, has been an immeasurable blessing and a daily reminder of life's unexpected gifts. She is, without a doubt, one of the greatest joys of my life and I tell her each and every day that she is my gift. I'm so grateful that I listened to my heart and my intuition.

I continued to work diligently at Chevron and earned another expatriate assignment, this time in Angola, Africa. I traveled back and forth for the first few years while waiting for my Visa to get approved. Finally, in August 2019, my son, daughter and I were officially en route to start our lives in one of the wealthiest countries in Africa. It was a chance to explore a new part of the world. From going on exciting safaris to learning Angola's official language, Portuguese, it was an amazing adventure! I even flew my parents out for an entire month to explore Cape Town, South Africa for Christmas and New Year's Eve.

Then the COVID pandemic hit, and life changed for everyone in every corner of the world. In March 2020, my assignment ended prematurely, and we had to come home. Although we weren't able to stay a full year, it still was an incredible, once-in-a-lifetime experience that I was able to share with my children and family. That is a huge blessing in itself.

During the pandemic, my sister and I took our mom on our first-ever mother-daughter trip to Jamaica. That time together allowed us to have some deep conversations that we never had before. I asked my mom, who was seventy-one-years-old at the time, if she could go back to her forty-year-old self, what would she tell herself? What was her dream? I asked my fifty-two-year-old sister the same thing. When I asked myself the same question, I realized that working for Chevron was never my dream. My dream was to travel, but I also loved business and making deals. I had always wanted to be one of the "sharks" on "Shark Tank" and invest in other companies.

Shortly after that trip, I attended a women's executive conference where Serena Williams was the keynote speaker. She spoke about Serena Ventures and *how only two percent of Venture Capital funds go to women and underrepresented founders. It was right then that I experienced another light bulb moment in my mind and heart. I knew that the universe was talking to me, telling me I had the skill set to close this gap.* I knew that with all I had learned throughout my career and education, I had the ability to have a positive impact on the world. I already navigated this challenging male-dominated energy industry, so when I heard only two percent of venture capital funds go to women, that fueled the fire in me. That meager number was absurd. I immediately started having conversations, and my computer must've heard me because an ad for Columbia Business School's Venture Capital and Private Equity Program popped up. I saw the ad and thought to myself, "You know, why not?" I needed to do it for my seventeen-year-old self who wanted to attend an Ivy League school like

Harvard. I was forty-two years old with no obstacles in my way and nothing holding me back. I applied and was accepted. I completed the course curriculum and graduated in the fall of 2023. While enrolling in Columbia, *I realized that I would always encourage my children and others to go for their dreams and that everyone should love what they do when they wake up in the morning. Yet I wasn't listening to my own advice. I wasn't chasing all my dreams.* I put in my two-week notice at Chevron and became the first Latina in Texas to launch a venture capital business - Dream Big Ventures.

Starting my own business has afforded me opportunities I would not have imagined. I've spoken at several global conferences from SXSW in Austin, Texas to the Women in Tech Texas with thousands of professional women in technology in attendance. My work has earned me various honors and awards such as the *Houston Business Journal Women Who Mean Business in Energy*, something I find very humbling.

I am very intentional about investing in women and underrepresented founders and helping others stand confidently in their power. I am a limited partner in four different funds, including Mendoza Ventures, Softeq, Portfolia, and Urban Capital Network. I am an angel investor with Angeles Investors and was named the Regional Lead for Texas and New Mexico. I am a shareholder in a women-owned bank, the first of its kind in the United States, called Agility Bank, and I am an investor in a women-owned winery and vineyard in California called Amadoras del Vino. This whole dream of mine has manifested in less than a year, and it has been such an incredibly fulfilling experience. *I wake up excited and fueled with energy because I really love what I do. I love knowing that I can help and make a difference in other women's lives. I've come to truly understand the power of connection.*

The experience I had at Chevron was invaluable and I am grateful, however, my ability to make a lasting impact in my community was limited. Since going out on my own, I have been able to expand my network and my associations to other women who are making $100 million in revenue, allowing me to continue to dream bigger, and that's key.

If there is one thing you can take away from my story, it is to stand confidently in your power while dreaming bigger. But the moment you feel like you've made it, it's time to reevaluate your goals and dreams and expand them even more.

No matter where you are right now or whatever is reflected in your bank account, it doesn't have to dictate where you're going or what you can do. It starts with your ability to imagine it. It's essential to be intentional about what you do with your time, associating with those you can learn from and who uplift you. There's never a dream that's too big or impossible, and the people you meet should help you believe this and tap into that growth mindset.

Big dreams will push you to level up, to learn about money, to invest in yourself, to be intentional about money and time, to continue to stay a student of life, and to do things differently than those around you. Bigger dreams enable us to break those generational cycles and to set ourselves and those coming after us up for success.

I dare you to take a moment right now and close your eyes. *Imagine your current dream multiplied by a hundred.* Hold that vision every day and believe me when I tell you it's possible- all of it. It's a matter of asking the right questions, knowing the right people, learning what you need to learn, and putting the necessary time in to make it happen. *The only question is, do you dare to dream bigger?*

GERARDO GARCIA-JURADO

Owner,
Eemageen, LLC

Gerardo, a Mexican immigrant, embarked on a transformative journey spanning two decades in the United States. Arriving in New York with dreams of conquering the corporate world, he navigated the intricacies of American culture and the challenges faced by the Hispanic community. Despite common immigration hurdles, Gerardo established a successful marketing career. His experiences underscore the need for support during the immigration process. With deep appreciation for family, hard work, optimism, and warmth, he passionately advocates for the Hispanic community's contributions to American society. Gerardo's story highlights the power of persistence and unity within diverse communities, inspiring others on their journeys.

Crossing Borders, Breaking Barriers:

A Latino Professional's Life in the U.S.

In the Beginning

Andrea, with her piercing gaze and steely resolve, took a long sip of her coffee before she said, "You'll never make it in a mainstream advertising agency here in the States." The sunlit café brimmed with the promise of new beginnings, but Andrea's prediction shadowed my optimism.

Fresh off the plane with only two weeks in New York under my belt, I found myself navigating the intricate web of American corporate culture. One acquaintance connected me with Andrea, an account director at a Hispanic ad agency. I needed to know the pulse of the industry, and she was to be my compass, but her candid advice was bitter to swallow. Time would prove her unsettling assertion to be painfully accurate.

Life's unpredictable winds had blown us into New York in the spring of 2000. It wasn't ambition but love. My brilliant wife had taken a prestigious assignment at the Mexican Foreign Trade Bank's N.Y. office. A temporary venture, we believed, but New York's irresistible pull meant that after an eight-year stint, the city's allure was too compelling to resist.

My heart raced at the prospect of conquering the Big Apple. It was the Colosseum of the modern world, where only the fiercest gladiators thrived. Having established my design firm, TOP MIND Visual Communications, in 1993, I was no stranger to adversity. By the turn of the millennium, TOP MIND had worked with giants like IBM and Hewlett-Packard. But New York required a different kind of resilience.

In this concrete jungle, I faced a bureaucratic paradox: I needed a job offer to get a work permit, yet no one would hire someone without one. My lack of experience with conventional employment meant that I was starting from scratch in a world I didn't understand. The internet was in its infancy in the year 2000, and that kind of information was not very accessible.

One anecdote exemplifies the cultural disparities I encountered. In those days, the internet was in its infancy, and only major corporations had websites. Designers like me carried oversized physical portfolios containing tangible samples of their finest work. When PepsiCo requested my portfolio, I insisted on presenting it in person. However, they insisted on postal submission, promising its return after review. This cultural misunderstanding cost me a valuable opportunity.

I could recount numerous similar stories.

Embracing Diversity

Another crucial aspect of my American experience was learning about the astonishing diversity in this great nation. Back in Mexico, we were all Mexicans, varying in complexion but united by nationality. However, America introduced me to the intricate tapestry of identities, races, and backgrounds that compose its population.

In the United States, individuals of Hispanic origin, hailing from diverse Latin American nations, are often collectively referred to as 'Mexicans' by those less informed, regardless of their true heritage. Puerto Ricans, some even Dominicans posing as Puerto Ricans due to their immigration path, thrive in numbers exceeding those on the island. The Cuban community is distinct, with some even eschewing the 'Hispanic' label in favor of 'Latino.' There are also Native Hispanics present on this land before the border shifted southward.

Let me pause here for an acknowledgment. I understand the over-simplification inherent in these comments, but they serve as a necessary backdrop for the stories I wish to share. As a Mexican, born and bred, I fall into the category of 'white' Mexicans, or as they are colloquially known, 'Whitexicans.' My fair complexion often prompts disbelief about my Mexican heritage, at least until I speak and reveal my unmistakable accent.

During a conversation with someone, I once mentioned my immigration from Mexico. To my surprise, he proclaimed that Mexicans were the most diligent, honest, and compassionate people in the U.S. At the time, I was a newcomer, and his comment struck me as peculiar. The stereotype of a lazy, dark-skinned Mexican slumbering under a sombrero beside a cactus and a donkey was the more prevalent image that comes to mind. This encounter opened my eyes to the untold stories of those who risked their lives crossing borders in pursuit of a better life for their families, dispelling the myth that immigrants come to be indolent or commit crimes. These courageous individuals arrive to work diligently, supporting their loved ones and striving for a brighter future. They may remain in the shadows, unacknowledged, but they might be one of American society's hardest-working, most honest, and compassionate members.

I was living in New York City when 9/11 unfolded—perhaps a story for another book. The official count stood at 2,977 lives lost, their faces etched into the heart-wrenching murals of missing persons adorning subway station walls. Yet, beneath the surface, hundreds of undocumented immigrants who toiled cleaning offices, preparing meals, and stocking shelves perished that day, their absence unmarked. Many had no families to mourn them, while others remained silent out of fear of government scrutiny.

Have you ever seen a memorial bearing their names? I haven't.

America's foundation is woven with the threads of immigrants. Every minority group has faced its share of challenges, be it the Irish, Italians, Asians, or Hispanics. They have encountered roadblocks along the way. However, my gaze turns to the Hispanic community today, especially those without legal status. They are the unsung heroes, warriors navigating a battlefield with no victory in sight. They resemble extras in a war film, soldiers fighting in the background while the hero claims the spotlight. They are indispensable, even if their names remain unknown, seemingly inconspicuous yet profoundly relevant.

Iván, a young and intelligent boy, was responsible for cleaning the offices where I worked in Manhattan. He sought solace in our conversations, recognizing me as the only one capable of understanding his experiences to some extent. He shared his harrowing journey across the border and how his mother had taken out a loan with a relative to pay a 'pollero' to smuggle him across the border. In the early 2000's, this journey came at a cost of $5,000. Every day, he toiled tirelessly to repay that debt.

He aspired to become a tattoo artist and open his own studio, driven by unwavering passion. He'd often declare, 'Un día, Gerardo, vas a ver' (One day, Gerardo, you'll see). I sincerely hope he has realized his dreams. Iván's story is but one of the countless narratives I've encountered since my arrival in the United States.

One late night/early morning, after revelry in Manhattan, my wife and I found ourselves at the only open establishment—a McDonald's. French fries replaced our customary Tacos Al Pastor, a testament to our adaptability. I spotted a Hispanic custodian vigorously mopping the floors. Engaging him in conversation, we connected. He asked about my occupation, and at that time, I was still on the hunt for my first job in the U.S.

I confessed my unemployed status, attributing it to the complexities I mentioned earlier. In a kind-hearted gesture, he offered to introduce me to 'his guy'—the one who could help me get a social security number and card, should I require one. I didn't need the card; I needed a job offer. Still, I appreciated his goodwill. He shared that he juggled two full-time jobs at different McDonald's locations, earning more than his compatriots because his English was a bit better. He resided in a rented two-bedroom apartment in Queens, housing nine other Mexican immigrants.

One remarkable facet of the Hispanic community is their unwavering support for one another in the United States.

My reminiscences of those New York days include visits to delis, often owned by Koreans but staffed predominantly by Mexicans. Their warmth and friendliness always struck me, and they'd often offer me 'pilón'—a little extra, a term from Mexico that encapsulates that extra touch of generosity.

During my tenure as the head of creative services at a branding firm in California, an encounter with Victor, the cleaning guy, left a lasting impression. While working late, he approached me one evening and inquired about my role at the agency. When I revealed that I oversaw the creative team, he asked, 'So, are you the boss of all these güeritos?' I affirmed, and he remarked, 'Wow, a Mexican can actually be the boss.' I've encountered many similar anecdotes over the years, reminding me of my impact on inspiring others despite my unique circumstances.

At this juncture, I must acknowledge my privilege. I was born into favorable circumstances, never experiencing hunger, jeopardy, or racial discrimination due to my skin color. I have a bachelor's and a master's degree. I grew up in a loving family, and my immigration to the United States was legal. Nevertheless, it was only upon moving here and witnessing the struggles of others that I truly comprehended my privileged background. Their stories of hardship fueled my desire to actively engage with the community, collaborating with Mexican Consulates, nonprofit organizations, and grassroots initiatives. My mission was to empower young immigrants to fight for their rights, pursue education, and become agents of positive change.

During my tenure at The Integer Group in Denver, I became acquainted with The Gold Crown Field House, an organization supported by the agency. Founded in 2003, it provides underprivileged children, primarily Hispanic and Black, with after-school programs to keep them engaged and off the streets while their parents work. Witnessing the intellect and passion within these young minds was deeply rewarding.

One memory that stands out is Michel's. Born to parents from Michoacán, Mexico, she aspired to design her own Quinceañera invitation. I worked with her for weeks, teaching her Photoshop so she could bring her vision to life.

Up to this point, I've mainly highlighted the experiences of undocumented immigrants, the most vulnerable group within the Hispanic community. Indeed, it is crucial to protect the weakest among us.

Now, let's shift our focus to those Hispanics born north of the border, along with their parents and grandparents. Many do not speak Spanish, even if it is their parents' native tongue. Some refrained from teaching their children Spanish, fearing it would lead to discrimination. Speaking Spanish carried a stigma back in the day, but I'm heartened to see the changing perception where multilingualism is celebrated.

Throughout my time in this remarkable country, I've had the privilege of meeting many individuals who possess a profound love for their culture—a sentiment I truly admire. It's humbling to acknowledge that they often have a deeper understanding of Latin American culture than I do myself. Take, for instance, Heather, a brilliantly gifted creative I had the pleasure of collaborating with.

Heather, who happens to be married to one of my closest Mexican-American friends, doesn't speak Spanish, but her mastery of Native Mexican dances and her extensive knowledge of pre-Colombian cultures surpass my own. Her unwavering passion for Mexican culture is nothing short of inspiring, and I've gleaned invaluable insights from her that I'll forever cherish.

Now, let's discuss the corporate Hispanic immigrants, as I like to call them. They are a group often overlooked. These immigrants, from various backgrounds, arrived in the United States legally, driven by diverse motivations. Their stories are not exclusive to Hispanics; they encompass Indians, Asians, and others who saw opportunities in the world's leading economy.

Resilience and Recognition

Our sojourn in the Tri-state area spanned eight years. While my wife served her role at the bank, I encountered my fair share of challenges. I must admit that I grappled with profound depression during this period, an unfamiliar battle. Finding my first job took over a year and a half. I cast a wide net, applying for any opportunity that crossed my path. At times, I felt unworthy, doubting that anyone would hire me. The few interviews I secured invariably hit a dead end when I revealed my lack of a work permit. It was a trying period, but I worked sporadically at trade shows, managing booths for Mexican companies and conducting cross-cultural presentations for expats and professionals.

In June of 2001, a breakthrough arrived when I interviewed at a Mid-Manhattan sales company seeking a Design Manager. The Asian lady who interviewed me did not pose the pivotal question about my work permit, and she hired me. However, a storm erupted when the subject surfaced as I filled out paperwork. She accused me of deception, asserting that I had lied to her. I corrected her, pointing out that she had never asked, and I had never told. I offered to work for free until my permit arrived. Fortunately, she agreed, and I was on legitimate footing within two weeks.

I remained with the company for over two years, working alongside a wonderful Jewish family. Their culture and the camaraderie of my Jewish coworkers provided invaluable insights. Puerto Rican colleagues added to the cultural mosaic with one Austrian friend, Kristian L., a funny and talented designer who ended up marrying a beautiful Mexican lady. This experience deepened my appreciation for diversity.

In 2004, we welcomed Fernando Garcia-Jurado into the world, our first and only child, a testament to our enduring legacy. His birth at Greenwich Hospital in Connecticut marked the end of one chapter and the beginning of another.

By the close of that year, I accepted a role as an art director at a promotional agency in Darien, CT, which had recently acquired the Cuauhtemoc-Moctezuma beer account in the U.S. This was the second-largest Mexican brewery, boasting a portfolio of prestigious beers. I spearheaded visual communication strategies for Tecate, Dos Equis, Bohemia, Sol, and Carta Blanca for nearly four years. A notable exception was my involvement in Dos Equis' The Most Interesting Man in the World campaign, targeting the general market.

Sadly, 2008 arrived, bringing news that my wife, Gaby, would be repatriated to Mexico. Our diplomatic status for the past eight years dictated this abrupt return. It was a trying period, especially for our son, Fernando. In general, we struggled to readapt. My wife experienced a harrowing armed robbery, and I faced challenges securing a well-paying job. The disparities between the two countries became glaringly evident. We felt like misfits, no longer belonging. It was a disheartening experience, prompting us to consider returning to the United States.

It took time, but eventually, I landed a position at the world's largest shopper marketing agency, based in Lakewood, CO. Initially, I oversaw the creative development for all of Kellogg's Hispanic promotions, continuing in the vein of serving the Hispanic market. Fortunately, my reputation as a strong leader reached the ears of the team overseeing the regional MillerCoors account. They were grappling with a period of low performance and approached me to join their team to boost morale and enhance design quality. This was a pivotal moment in my career as it allowed me to showcase my talent in the general market, breaking the spell that had been cast upon me.

A pivotal moment arrived when my immigration status became precarious due to a layoff resulting from the MillerCoors account's loss.

I found myself unemployed and, subsequently, lost my work visa. To clarify, a work visa is essential for legal employment in the United States as a non-permanent resident, often obtained through company sponsorship. In my case, my visa sponsorship had been withdrawn. Thankfully, my wife had already begun working for a restaurant group, allowing her to transfer my visa to hers as a dependent. While this meant I was allowed to remain in the country, I couldn't work anymore.

To keep myself engaged while seeking employment with sponsorship, I collaborated with a Denver-based Hispanic agency to create a PSA-based campaign for the Colorado Department of Transportation, focusing on preventing driving under the influence. This campaign earned our team an Emmy® in 2017, a cherished achievement among my professional accolades.

Eventually, I was hired by a branding company in the Bay Area that was willing to sponsor me, and we relocated in late 2017. My role involved overseeing the agency's entire creative development. Importantly, my immigration attorney informed me that I could apply for a Green Card under the self-petition status, citing my extraordinary abilities and professional trajectory. My application was approved, fundamentally altering our lives. After years of uncertainty, our future in the United States was secure.

Today

More recently, I have launched my own practice, focusing on assisting mission-driven brands and organizations in developing community and environmentally-oriented campaigns for nonprofits. For two years, I have had the privilege of serving as the president of the American Marketing Association in San Francisco, striving to support the Bay Area community and nurture the next generation of marketers, all while championing diversity, equity, and inclusion.

Among various endeavors, and perhaps one that fills me with immense enthusiasm, I initiated a nonprofit organization, Marketing for All. The core mission of this organization is to propel local communities towards prosperity through economic development, achieved by providing heavily subsidized, top-notch marketing services.

After over two decades of residing here and navigating through various immigration statuses, I'm delighted to announce that I became a U.S. citizen just a month ago (August 2023). Today, I take immense pride in embracing my identity as a Mexican-American—a Hispanic residing in the United States. I firmly believe that our culture has enriched America. Our core values—family, hard work, optimism, and warmth—have played an integral role in shaping this great nation.

We continually demonstrate our worth by supporting one another, respecting diverse cultures and religions, advocating for our rights, pursuing education, and contributing to our communities. It's a value that is sometimes overlooked but remains an undeniable force in the American tapestry.

I am deeply honored and humbled to be part of this editorial project alongside extraordinary individuals—community leaders, entrepreneurs, scientists, and more- who have been at the forefront of the cultural transformation in modern America. They reaffirm daily that Hispanics are essential to our society and economy.

In gratitude and with hope.

PEDRO DAVID ESPINOZA

CEO,
Pan Peru U.S.A.

Pedro David Espinoza is a TED speaker, entrepreneur, investor, and author. As the founder of SmileyGo and Pan Peru U.S.A., Pedro has significantly influenced the tech and social sectors. In 2019 he authored "Differences That Make a Difference" and received the Latin International Book Award for #1 Business Book. A prolific keynote speaker and startup investor, Pedro has spoken at companies such as PwC, UBS & GE and contributed to startups like KiwiBot, MoCaFi, NadineWest, Noyo, Paladin, & Feed.fm. His leadership roles and advisory positions focus on impacting Hispanic leadership in technology.

Failing Forward

What is life without faith besides the fleeting nature of existence that ends when our physical bodies are gone? While it may be acceptable to focus on personal and professional achievements, I believe that dedicating oneself to something greater, something with lasting significance beyond a mere few decades is the key to true success. As I share my thoughts, I am unreservedly open about my Christian faith, for I believe that Christ is the foundation of all my actions and accomplishments. It is to Him that I attribute all credit and praise.

I grew up in Peru with two engineers as my parents. They divorced when my sisters and I were young, so I spent most of my time with my mother. My mother taught me everything I know, but most importantly she taught me that the MOST POWERFUL force is not the speed of light nor the speed of sound but is the power of will. My mother wasn't the only powerful woman who raised me as a child. My two sisters were outstanding students who greatly inspired me. Karina attended Stanford and is now a medical doctor. My oldest sister, Dianna was the first one in the family to pursue a higher education in the United States, receive merit-based scholarships, studied abroad in China learning Mandarin Chinese and later went on to be a successful marketing manager. In fact, in Peru it was common to see powerful women everywhere. When the time came for me to move to Silicon Valley, I was taken aback by the lack of women and overall diversity of those in power. Despite being the hub of innovation in the U.S., there were more CEOs named John than there were Hispanic CEOs in the tech industry. Shocked by this stark contrast and inspired by the powerful women in my life, I was inspired to write my first book,

"Differences that Make a Difference," which delves into the significance of diversity in entrepreneurship and amplifies the voices of diverse thought leaders.

Following in the footsteps of my sister Karina, the expectations were high for me as I went through school. However, in high school I decided to drop out of the International Baccalaureate (IB) when I was just sixteen. A faculty member from my school told me that I wouldn't get into college without those classes and even suggested that I stay in Peru rather than going to school in the U.S. However, I've always believed that education is not a one-size-fits-all approach and that it can be nonlinear. Despite that faculty member's discouragement, I took a step back to figure out what worked best for me, taking easier classes, and improving my GPA. I used my extra time, high energy, and curiosity, to help other students. Dropping out of IB allowed me to preside over the Business Honor Society, the Music Honor Society, and get elected to Student Body Government. I had the time to dedicate to the five instruments played and since my parents wanted me to work starting at 16 years old, I did just that. I got my hands dirty and organized impact trips to help people in my mom's village, Pampas Grande, located in the Peruvian mountains. I started fundraising to provide the kids in Pampas Grande with access to computers, and now, 15 years later, some of them are in college pursuing careers in entrepreneurship, arts, and music. Despite not having the best GPA and not taking honors or full AP/IB courses, I still managed to get accepted to Berkeley for my undergraduate studies with merit-based scholarships by focusing on what worked for me.

In my first year of college, I realized that I didn't have the same network connections as many of my peers. While they had family members working at companies like Google, Cisco, and VMware, I didn't have that advantage. I applied to numerous internships but was rejected by companies like McKinsey, Deloitte, and Apple. Instead of giving up, I decided to take matters into my own hands and work for myself. I saw an opportunity to apply for a program at Stanford called the Engineering Technology Entrepreneurship Program. Despite facing rejection from a specific class, I wanted to take, I was determined to get in. I reached out to the professor multiple times but received no response. So, I took matters into my own hands and waited outside his office for an hour. When he finally arrived, I had four minutes to convince him why I should be allowed into his class. I gave him my elevator pitch, sharing my vision, resilience, and determination. He recognized my drive and decided to make an exception for me. This opportunity led me to start my own company, Smiley Go, at the age of nineteen. Which got me accepted to a Stanford management science & engineering program: technology entrepreneurship. Smiley Go became a part of Univision and even made an appearance on Shark Tank. I raised capital and expanded to thirty countries across five continents, gaining press coverage along the way. It has been an incredible journey, filled with joy and learning from failures. I've done a TED talk on building relational bridges because it truly is through authentic connections that create meaningful relationships that can elevate us to the next level in our lives.

While in school, I was honored to receive the Cal Alumni Association (CAA) Leadership Award and the Jack Larson Scholarship Award, as well as the Seed Funding Grant by the Berkeley Haas Dean Startup award to attend Berkeley. During the scholarship luncheon at Berkeley, where there were 300 donors and students, the president of the CAA asked for a student to give a speech thanking the donors. To my surprise, not one person raised their hand. Even though English wasn't my first language, I decided to take the opportunity and volunteered to speak. I thanked the donors and shared my Peruvian immigrant story. I shared with the crowd about my parents' upbringings in the Andes mountains and Amazon rainforest. Perhaps to others, standing up and holding that mic to speak in front of hundreds of Berkeley students and distinguished alumni may not have seemed like that big of a deal but to me, it was meaningful. As a child I had been ashamed of my Incan Quechua native roots, but now speaking about my family's origins brought into perspective the progression and the importance of continuing to push myself. It was bigger than me. It was then that I also recognized the importance of being proud of our culture and background. Later, when Janet Napolitano, the former U.S. Secretary of Homeland Security, President of the University of California, and governor of Arizona, awarded me the Entrepreneur of the Year I spoke proudly spoke of my Incan roots during my speech. Now, when I attend events like the World Economic Forum in Davos and meet CEOs from around the world, I love to share about Peru's rich culture, history, and attractions. I talk about Machu Picchu, penguins in the Ballestas Islands, our beautiful beaches in Piura, the world's deepest canyon (Colca), and the highest navigable lake in the world: Titicaca. I want everyone to know that being proud of where we come from makes us more authentic, and it can help us succeed in life.

The Bible teaches us the importance of having a cheerful heart and surrounding ourselves with encouraging people. Early in my undergraduate studies, as a good STEM student I took multivariable calculus, but I faced challenges while taking the 8 A.M. class that led me to have to retake the course. One morning, I overslept, and I confess, I had to choose between attending class or having breakfast. I decided to have breakfast at the Golden Bear Cafe in Berkeley instead. I walked into the diner filled with Berkeley students except for one older man with gray hair having breakfast by himself. I was intrigued as to who he was and went up to his table and told him that he looked like he's an important person and asked if I could have breakfast with him. Frank was his name, and it turned out that I was right, he was an important person. I noticed that he was wearing a Latin American flag pin, and I asked him about it. He explained that he used to be the ambassador to Uruguay under President Bush. We clicked and started speaking in Spanish, despite our differences in political affiliation, religion, ethnicity, mother tongue, zip code, and net worth. It was a connection between an eighty-four-year-old and a nineteen-year-old from completely different backgrounds. We bonded over our shared language which he learned while living in Uruguay. At the end of our conversation, he gave me his business card and I shared that I was a FinTech entrepreneur. He revealed that he was the retired chairman and CEO of Jefferies, one of the largest investment banks in the world. Can you believe that he became the first investor in my tech startup two years later? It just goes to show the power of relationships.

Another time after a speech, a donor can up to me asking if I played golf. Instead of declining, I simply asked her to teach me. She didn't hesitate but instead graciously agreed. I borrowed golf accessories from my friends and bought cheap golf balls from Walmart and Costco. The following week, I played golf with Rosemary and discovered that her cousin was from Germany. I had studied German for two years at Berkeley and spoke four languages, so we bonded over our shared interest in languages. Through Rosemary, I also met her son, Eric, who was an executive at Adobe. Five years later, Adobe was the first tech company to host my first book talk: Differences That Make a Difference tour. This experience taught me the importance of connecting with people, following up, and gaining sponsors who support and vouch for you in various settings, such as the boardroom and hiring room.

In the speeches I've given on the importance of building relationships and networks, I suggest to the audience to draw three circles: operational, personal, and strategic. The operational circle represents your day-to-day interactions. For example, if you're a wealth advisor, this would include other financial advisors. If you're a software engineer, it would include other programmers. If you're a CEO, it would include other CEOs. The personal circle consists of people from your church, family, synagogue, running club, tennis club, neighborhood, and so on. Lastly, the strategic circle represents who you aspire to be in the future. For instance, if you're a finance intern, you may want to become a CFO when you're fifty-five years old. If you're a software engineer, you may aim to be a CTO. If you work in Hollywood, you may aspire to be someone like Chris Pratt. If you're an NCAA tennis player, you may want to be like Novak Djokovic. It's about envisioning where you see yourself ten to twenty years from now. In my speeches, I always encourage people to identify a critical connection within each circle and reach out to them. You don't need a title to be a leader, and you don't have to be a millionaire to help a millionaire. Ask them how you can help and serve them because our culture tends to focus on taking rather than giving. The Bible teaches us the importance of generosity, serving others, and loving one another, rather than solely focusing on ourselves, our lives, our families, or our net worth. My first book is a prime example of just how powerful this practice is. I can't reiterate enough that I came to the U.S. with zero network, and a handful of years later I was able to interview 100 CEOs for my first book: Differences That Make a Difference. That doesn't happen by chance or by having a mindset focusing on what can I get out of a relationship.

In 2018, I had the opportunity to attend a conference in San Francisco called TBC (Transform the Bay with Christ). The keynote speaker was Pat Gelsinger, the CEO of VMware at the time. His speech was truly inspiring, and I was in awe of his accomplishments as a Fortune 500 CEO. After his speech, many people wanted to take selfies and get autographs from him. I was faced with a dilemma because I was hungry and wanted to grab dinner, but I also wanted to meet Pat. Being a Peruvian, I decided to trust in the Lord and believe that I would find a way to meet him later. The next day, I purchased Pat's book, "The Juggling Act," and read it. I was impressed by his faith and his support for girls in Kenya. He climbed Mt. Kilimanjaro to build high schools and computer labs for girls! I also learned that he was the first CTO of Intel and had attended Stanford University. So, I took a chance and sent him an email. I didn't have his exact email address, so I sent ten emails to different variations of his name @vmware.com. To my surprise, one email went through, and nine emails bounced. My message was short and sweet. I introduced myself as a Christ-centered entrepreneur, immigrant founder, and startup CEO who admired his work and wanted to learn from his core values. To my amazement, Pat replied to me the next day at 5 A.M., as he is also an early riser. He invited me to his office in Palo Alto for a ten-minute meeting. The only problem was that I lived in Pleasant Hill, which was not a short distance away. However, I was determined and willing to make the journey.

When the day came, I must admit I was a bit too excited. After all, Pat was a Fortune 500 CEO and a multimillionaire. However, as soon as I arrived, I realized that we had more in common than I had expected. He was also a morning person, loved to exercise, and was learning Chinese! He was the grandfather of a Latino boy. We bonded over our shared love for Latin heritage. Our faith in Christ also brought us closer together, as we adhered to the same Christ-centered principles of servant leadership, generosity, and boldness. Despite our differences in age and background, we connected on a deeper level through our shared values. Pat's wealth and status didn't matter at that moment. What mattered were the values he embodied, such as generosity, love, faith, and hope. We became friends and Pat wrote the foreword for my first book. Pat's connections and support have opened doors for me and have allowed me to learn that it's never too late to pursue their dreams.

I believe it's never too late for anyone to pursue their goals and dreams. Different people have different timelines for success. For example, Barack Obama became president at the age of forty-six, while Donald Trump became president at the age of seventy. When Novak Djokovic hit his early 20's, Roger Federer and Rafael Nadal were dominating men's tennis. Later on, Djokovic would surpass both as the man with the most slams. It's important to remember that everyone has their own strengths and weaknesses. Although I experienced early success as an immigrant at the age of nineteen, I believe that anyone can start their journey towards success today.

Discipline has played a significant role in my life, and I credit my mother for instilling a strong sense of discipline in me. I'm grateful that I have never needed coffee. I don't drink alcohol. My parents raised me with tons of fruits and vegetables, no TV during the week, and a lot of sports. Dad would always teach me to wake up early at 6:00 A.M. with no alarms. I grew up in Peru with taking cold showers. To this day, I still shower with cold water, and I love it. When I saw the students taking steaming hot showers in the dorms when I first came to the U.S., I didn't understand it. Through my experiences of the two different cultures and countries, it seems to me that a lot of the youth have become accustomed to comfort and it's proven to be the biggest distraction. Therefore, I would encourage anyone who hasn't taken full advantage of the opportunities in the United States to reflect on their habits and make positive changes. Time is incredibly valuable, and it's important to be mindful of how we spend it. Small habits, such as excessive time spent on platforms like Netflix, TikTok, Instagram, YouTube, or Amazon, can accumulate and take away from more productive pursuits. It's essential to evaluate where we invest our time and make conscious choices. The Bible says in Proverbs 4:23, "Above all else, guard your heart. It is the wellspring of life." Our body is the temple of the Holy Spirit, so when we continue to allow ourselves to become addicted to substances or social media, it blocks us from being fully guided by the Holy Spirit. Instead of complaining about a lack of time, we should consider how we can prioritize our activities. Taking risks and having faith in oneself, regardless of what previous outcomes we've experienced, are crucial steps towards personal growth and success. This is what I call failing forward, and it truly is the way to sustainable success.

MARCIA V. MORENO

President,
AmMore Consulting, LLC

Marcia's journey is truly an American story - a North and South American one. Born and raised in Chile, she came to the U.S. in 2005 to pursue her graduate studies and has lived here since. The immigrant experience demonstrated to Marcia firsthand what it means to not feel included and not be heard - which informs her work. Blending her personal experience with her professional expertise, she now makes it her mission to pave a better road for up-and-coming Latino talent, including her bilingual 11-year-old.

In 2018, she founded AmMore Consulting, to focus her passion for elevating Cleveland's Latino professionals and helping organizations get Latino Ready™. AmMore is committed to creating more diverse, inclusive, and equitable workplaces by supporting organizations to develop long-lasting strategies and systems to effectively attract, recruit and retain Latino talent to succeed and thrive.

AMORE:

Our Stories Connect Us

In a world filled with endless possibilities, it is the people we encounter along our journey who truly shape our lives by igniting our passions that ultimately awaken our true selves. It is in the journey with people, in every capacity, that propels us towards greatness. The happiness and hurt they bring serve a purpose in reaching our destiny when we allow it. Yet, more importantly, it is the connection that we hold with ourselves that is the most powerful. In our journey, we allow people and circumstances to take our power away, the power of having a choice. It is through this self-imposed prison that is ultimately the catalyst of our liberation. It always unfolds differently in everyone's life, some end up resigning and settling for the prison, while others dare to escape into the unknown. Six years in entrepreneurship, as a first-generation Latina in the United States, I celebrate all the pivotal moments with people in my professional and personal life that led me to where I am today.

I was born in 1978 in Talca, Chile, during the dictatorship of Pinochet. Despite the repression, my parents, who worked in the public sector, provided us with stability. We lived a regimented life with limited options for entertainment and groceries. However, I didn't fully realize the extent of these restrictions until college. My parents emphasized education, and I attended an all-girls Catholic school with strict rules. If I didn't bring home perfect grades, my parents would have serious conversations with me. Growing up in a small town, everyone knew everything about everyone, and my father's position at the hospital made me feel like I was constantly being watched. I had a free spirit that clashed with my parents' more conservative approach to family. After high school, I wanted to experience life away from the rules and pressure. I was accepted in a big university in Chile, away from home, and studied journalism for five years. Through a partnership between my university and a college in Ohio, I was able to participate in an exchange program and receive a full scholarship for my master's degree in the United States.

When an immigrant arrives in the United States, the journey is filled with countless challenges, even for those who speak some English, like myself. While my English skills were decent, I struggled to express myself in the same way I could in Spanish. The differences extended beyond language, encompassing every aspect of daily life. Imagine arriving as an adult with just two suitcases and a single friend who had come before me. I had to navigate finding an apartment, paying for classes, setting up utilities, getting a phone, opening a bank account - all as an international person in a country that doesn't fully understand the immigrant experience. The challenges were endless. From the countless documents required for simple tasks like getting a library card to the concept of credit scores and taxes, everything felt like a monumental hurdle. In 2005, cell phones weren't as widely available, so even making a simple call to my family required purchasing a card from a convenience store and finding a pay phone. And to top it all off, people constantly pointed out my accent, while I struggled to understand their own accents. To make matters worse, hardly anybody made an effort to bridge the communication gap, leaving me feeling isolated and unheard. This experience left a scar in my spirit that, years later, has helped fuel my purpose as a consultant to help companies become what I call, "Latino-ready." What this calls for is a greater sense of inclusivity and a deeper understanding of our ethnic group's complexity and richness. Companies need to recognize that their practices, whether intentional or not, may not resonate with us or make us feel included. Yet, this was only the beginning of my experiences of feeling like an outsider and isolated in the United States.

Despite the challenges, I have come to appreciate Cleveland as an "acquired taste" - the city that welcomed me and I made home, but still in need of greater inclusion.

Drawing from my own experiences, I can empathize with my clients and provide valuable insights. I have a vast network of friends and colleagues from Latin America who share similar experiences and challenges. I bring this collective voice to my clients, presenting them with data that highlights the importance of diversity and inclusion in the workplace. I emphasize that creating an environment where everyone can thrive is not only the right thing to do but also essential for future success in a changing demographic landscape. Additionally, my expertise in talent and workforce development allows me to offer practical solutions based on real experiences and ongoing issues. By leveraging my lived experience as a Latina professional, I can advocate for meaningful change and help organizations create a more inclusive and supportive work environment.

I established my company, AmMore Consulting, in 2018 after leaving a position at a big law firm due to stress and mistreatment. My company was born from my experiences of feeling unseen and unheard, with the goal of creating a platform to support others in similar situations. Quitting my job was a tough decision, as I had always been focused on my career and never considered being a stay-at-home parent. However, the demanding nature of my job and the desire to be present for my son led me and my husband to make a hard choice. During my time at home, I engaged in self-reflection and various activities to discover my goals and values. I also sought feedback from friends, colleagues, and mentors through informational interviews. Their insights helped shape my next steps. While I initially resisted the idea of becoming a coach or consultant, multiple Latina leaders suggested that I pursue consulting due to my unique experiences in the U.S. working in non-profits as well as the corporate world as a Latina. These suggestions made me reflect on my own experiences as a Latina professional and inspired me to start my consulting business, AmMore Consulting on July 19, 2018.

From a young age, I had a strong desire to help others who, like me, longed for a sense of belonging and a tight-knit community. I wanted to connect with individuals who were facing similar challenges and provide them with the support they needed. However, I soon realized that it was equally important for organizations and employers to understand the value of having Latinos in their workforce. At that time, I lacked the knowledge and awareness that I now possess.

Through extensive research and personal experiences, I have come to understand the complexities that arise from cultural differences, particularly for those who were born and raised in other countries. The historical and cultural factors in the United States play a significant role in shaping these challenges. These challenges, I discovered, were not only external but also internal. As an individual, I needed to identify the key factors that would contribute to my success in the workplace. This realization became the foundation that AmMore was built on, to make organizations, both for-profit and nonprofit, "Latino ready."

There's a significant amount of work that needs to be done for companies to truly understand the intricacies of diversity and its impact on their efforts to foster inclusivity and hire a more diverse workforce. When everything is measured with a single yardstick, it becomes easy to dismiss those who don't fit the mold as being wrong or inadequate in some way, whether it's their language skills, communication style, or even their processes. This often leads to a feeling that you have to constantly prove yourself, going above and beyond expectations, and yet still not receiving the recognition or validation deserved.

The truth is, no matter how much you accomplish, it never seems to be enough. For example, as a journalist with a strong background in Spanish grammar, I faced my own set of challenges when working at the law firm, with every email being scrutinized and criticized by a group of attorneys because I used a comma instead of a period. These experiences were incredibly difficult for me. However, they also served as a catalyst for my journey. I realized that I wanted to create a space where individuals like me could feel a sense of belonging and find others who were facing similar struggles. Simultaneously, I recognized the need to educate organizations and employers about the value of having Latinos in their workforce. At that time, I didn't fully understand the complexities of cultural and historical factors that influenced these challenges, but through continuous learning and research, I gained a deeper understanding.

99.9% of the people I know are Latinos like me, and most of them have advanced degrees or at least an undergraduate education. Contrary to popular belief, there are educated Latinos who speak both English and Spanish and have legal documentation. While there is still work to be done in terms of increasing educational levels within the community, the notion that qualified Latinos are nowhere to be found is simply not aligned with my experience. And the opportunity arose in 2020, amid the pandemic when I found myself stuck at home with not much going on, I realized that I needed to take advantage of the situation and do something to remain relevant as a business and fulfill an idea I had in mind for years. With some of my clients deciding to pause their engagements, I had the time to dedicate to this endeavor.

Although I initially felt like I didn't have all the pieces together and usually preferred to have everything in place before launching something, I learned that sometimes things have a way of working themselves out. So, I reached out to my close friends in the community, the ones I knew would believe in me and trust what I was going to do. I invited them to be part of this platform, which at that point was just a dream and a vision without a name. After receiving around 110 applications and pictures, I formed my first cohort and called it the 100+ Latinos Cleveland Must Know. I set the timeline to launch it during Hispanic Heritage Month, but I didn't have any help as I do now with subsequent cohorts. So, the night before the launch, I stayed up all night creating social media posts, wording templates, a media package, and a kit for each Latino to share on their own social media. Meanwhile, I reached out to the media and prepared to publish the list on my website.

I remember sitting on the first floor of my house, working tirelessly until five A.M. when the emails were scheduled to go out. I went to bed and woke up around nine A.M. to an explosion of missed calls from the media and hundreds of posts on Facebook and LinkedIn. It was truly unbelievable and overwhelming. Finally, there was a way for us to show that we exist, that we are here, that we are valuable, and that we are proud of who we are. It was an incredible feeling to witness the power of community and the sense of recognition and visibility it brought to individuals. For me, it was a phenomenon that began to take on a life of its own. The media started referring to it as something extraordinary. It was truly mind-boggling. Each year, I make it a point to create a new group of 100 individuals for the 100+ Latinos to further raise awareness and foster a sense of community and visibility. This program primarily serves as a marketing initiative to provide stability and support to individuals who, like me, aspire to achieve great things. When people claim that they can't find lawyers, business owners, accountants, or engineers, we prove them wrong. We are right here, ready to be seen, heard, and valued. Ready to lead and change the world.

The 100+ Latinos platform proved to have a visible impact on people's lives. I learned of a young man who was studying at Cleveland State University at the time and was actively searching for a job. After becoming a part of the 100+ Latinos list, he began connecting with other members and eventually found his first job as a community organizer at the Young Latino Network. He recognized me and approached me at an event, expressing his gratitude for the 100+ Latinos platform. He credited it for helping him discover the organization and ultimately securing his desired job in his desired field. This job opportunity was previously unknown to him before being reached out to the organization. The visibility and openness to creating connections that the platform provides have led to the formation of valuable connections and collaborations. Other organizations are also taking notice of the list, resulting in a synergy that is positively transforming the city. While I am proud to be a driving force behind this transformation, I also hope that these individuals will pay it forward by supporting and empowering others, as that is the essence of the platform - to be a catalyst for positive change.

Then there is Christina, who works at a local nonprofit in a nearby city. She discovered her community and realized that there were other Mexican Americans in the region who shared similar struggles and experiences. Prior to this, she had never found someone in her area who was educated and going through similar challenges. She referred to finding her people and went on to create a mini-chapter of the 100+ Latinos in Akron, which is about 45 minutes south of Cleveland. This chapter provided a space for them to connect, engage in professional development, participate in civic activities, and collaborate with nonprofits in need of support. Christina's initiative and the creation of this group showcase her dedication and commitment to amplifying efforts and making a difference.

Linda is another example of the impact my company has had on the community. She was a newcomer to Cleveland, facing numerous challenges in her personal life. When she reached out to me, she expressed doubts about her qualifications and whether she belonged in the network. Despite going through a difficult time, she had a strong desire to connect with others and start her own business. Three years later, she is now a member of my second cohort and has successfully established her own business. She has found her community, gained confidence, and is actively involved in various activities. She has shared with me that being part of the 100+ Latinos has given her a sense of purpose, pride, and self-respect that she previously lacked. These stories of personal transformation and growth make me incredibly proud because it shows that this platform is making a real impact on individuals. By changing the lives of individuals, I believe we can ultimately change the world, creating a multiplying effect.

I provide various monthly programs for professionals and leadership development, as well as assistance with skills, networking, and connecting with companies and human resources for employment opportunities. Throughout the year, I collaborate with different partners to offer these services. Currently, my business has 400 participants in the program. Although this program doesn't generate much revenue for me, I have invested countless hours in recruiting, connecting with people, attending events, and ensuring that we are reaching those who are seeking support. While my business may be a small community, I am determined to make a difference and provide a space where individuals can truly be themselves and feel a sense of belonging. It brings me joy to know that I have positively impacted people's lives through this program, and I wish there had been something similar available when I first started. That's the essence of what I'm aiming to achieve.

The concept of authenticity has become quite cliché nowadays, with everyone emphasizing the need to be true to oneself. While I do believe it is important because it's been a significant aspect of my own life as well. However, reaching that point of authenticity requires embarking on a personal journey of self-discovery. It is not something that comes naturally or can be easily defined.

It involves deep self-reflection and the understanding that one's identity is not static, but rather constantly evolving. It's important to participate in this part of your journey with a goal and intention. The definition of success is unique to each individual and can change over time. It is important to be open to different interpretations of success and not compare yourself to others. Personal experiences, such as leaving a job or going through a divorce, can lead to feelings of failure, but it is crucial to reflect and recognize your own accomplishments. Success should be measured by your own standards and can vary at different stages of life. For me, success means having the freedom and independence to choose how I spend my time. However, it's taken most of my life to get to this point of knowing who I am and what I want and not trying to get into places where I don't belong or cannot be myself. Life is just too short to spend it in places that do not value you. My hope is for my business to help others create this reality in their own lives by facilitating a place for people to come together.

HEALTH & WELLNESS

SAUL GOMEZ

Humanist & Inclusion Optimization Expert

Saul was born in South Central Los Angeles and is a retired Navy Chief with 24 years of service. He was the Chief Diversity Officer and Leading Chief of Strategic Innovation for a 59k-person organization.

He holds a degree in business & human resource management and is a Certified Diversity Professional (CDP), a Certified Project Director (CPD), an Agile HR Professional (ICP-AHR), and a certified professional coach.

He is a graduate of the Defense Equal Opportunity Management Institute and is pursuing a doctoral degree in Organizational Change and Leadership at the University of Southern California's Rossier School of Education.

ZION

The Dwelling Place of God

I'm a 100% disabled combat veteran and a director at a consulting firm where I find great joy in the work I do. I retired from the military in 2020 after twenty-four years of service. I joined the Navy to box and after reporting to my first duty station, I was informed that I couldn't box for the Navy because I was slated to deploy. Upset and disappointed, I intended to leave the service after my enlistment, however, the events of 9/11 spawned the beginning of an unforgettable career.

During the early stages of the war in 2002, I was deployed to Kuwait, where we escorted cargo ships on their way to the port of Umm-Qasr, in Iraq. I also participated in counterdrug operations, working with South American Special Forces in search of drug runners and semi-submersible submarines used to transport cocaine. In the Middle East, I conducted detainee operations, movement control, and various other assignments across Kuwait, Iraq, Afghanistan, and the United Arab Emirates. One of the most significant deployments I experienced was my 13th and final one. I oversaw manpower, and movement control, and served as the Navy element Senior Enlisted Advisor in Kabul, Afghanistan – my boss, a two-star general, was killed by an insurgent ambush, along with twenty-five others, critically injured. These types of deployments gradually shaped my jaded outlook on humanity, and throughout my journey of healing, I've learned that sometimes things must fall apart so that they can be put back together, stronger, and more resilient than before.

I was diagnosed with PTSD (Post-Traumatic Stress Disorder) in 2015 after struggling to adjust to being home again. Deployments felt more comfortable than being home, and after each deployment, my wife would notice changes in me. I became disassociated, developed a short fuse, and was constantly on edge, unable to sleep, completely fixated on work and the next deployment. From my deployments, however, I would bring home that operational mindset, which negatively impacted my family. It got to the point where my wife would gauge my mood when I got home before letting our kids interact with me - they were on pins and needles whenever I was around. I felt anxious and unable to focus, and my demeanor toward them was coarse. I struggled with disassociation, depression, and nightmares. I would zone out for extended periods; often my wife would sleep in a different room due to my trauma-related nightmares. It was a manifestation of the lifetime accumulation of trauma that I had compartmentalized for so long. Not being able to deploy anymore, I no longer had an outlet and became absent, physically there, yet mentally checked out.

One of my darkest moments was the evening I nearly lost my oldest son Zion – he was fifteen at the time. I came home from work late, put my bag down, and proceeded into the kitchen. Zion was wrestling at the time and wanted to show me what he learned. Without notice, he jumped on my back, and I blacked out. Muscle memory took over and when I came to, I was on top of him, one knee on his stomach and my forearm across his neck. While trying to figure out how I got there, I realized I was reaching for where I would normally keep my knife or a pistol. By that time, I had removed all weapons from the house. It was undoubtedly a difficult time for them, as they witnessed firsthand the toll that my PTSD had taken on our family. I am eternally grateful for their unwavering support, love, and resilience.

Being diagnosed with PTSD I was placed on Limited Duty, a status given when service members are incapacitated and unable to deploy. My job shifted to a very corporate-like environment in the HR field. I transitioned into a desk job as a senior advisor, overseeing the Military Equal Opportunity Program, with twelve direct reports serving an enterprise of 59,000 personnel across the nation. This was a significant culture shock for me, and I struggled to adjust. Unfortunately, I was removed from that position due to my lack of diplomacy and awareness of office politics - I was regarded as coarse, intimidating, and combative.

I was placed in a less prominent role within the organization, referred to as the "junk drawer," where I could be tucked away in a corner. During this time, I discovered and became fascinated with the Centers for Adaptive Warfighting (CAW), a military entity leveraging agile modalities to solve complex problems. From that junk drawer, I became a facilitator for the CAW, and the Chief Diversity Officer for the organization. Despite this, in 2020, four months before my retirement, I felt out of place - reminiscent of my childhood fantasies of being rescued from a world that I didn't belong to. I reached a point where I even felt out of place in the military. I felt lost – and apathetic about life and attempted suicide by taking as many prescription pills as I could. I woke up eighteen hours later, angry that I had survived. When I was ready, I sought help, never realizing how much I needed it until I got it.

The journey to where I am now was not an easy one, yet worth it. It involved a steep fall and numerous subsequent challenges that ultimately led me to where I am today. The gifts of adversity taught me how to compartmentalize at a young age, because of the traumatic experiences I faced early on in my life. One vivid memory that stands out is witnessing my father physically abuse my mother by taking a cast iron skillet upside her head. I was only three years old at the time and remember feeding my younger sister next to my mom while she lay on the kitchen floor unconscious. When my father returned home hours later, it was as if nothing had happened. This early exposure to domestic violence caused me to compartmentalize my emotions and experiences - something that later became a curse and a blessing. Growing up in South Central

Los Angeles, I was exposed to gangs and violence, witnessing my first murder at the age of fourteen. A kid from my neighborhood was shot in the back fleeing from a rival drug dealer, and then nine more times in the head once he collapsed. I had guns pulled on me and even saw a person die from a shotgun wound to the stomach. These incidents normalized violence for me and reinforced my ability to compartmentalize.

Attempting to provide me with a better environment, my mother sent me to a magnet school in the Valley. To further keep me away from the streets, she enrolled me in a youth program called the Sheriff's Explorer Program. During a ride along, we were dispatched to a shooting at a nightclub; I was to cordon the area to keep the public away from contaminating the crime scene and check on victims. As I approached one victim, I watched him take his last breath of life in a pool of blood from the close-range shotgun wound to his stomach. I didn't feel sad or afraid – I was numb, indifferent, and didn't understand why.

The experiences I had growing up primed me well for the military. There were rival Mexican gangs, as well as Bloods and Crips, which are gangs with predominantly Black members. I lived in a different neighborhood than the school I attended. One Mexican gang would chase me on my way to school so they could jump me, while another gang near my school would chase me on my way home from school - all because I wouldn't join their gang. It was a constant struggle, always running to stay safe, head on a swivel – and it kept me alive.

I would get bullied in school and vividly recall an incident in eighth grade where a Black student, who I later found out was a Blood, stood up for me and put an end to the bullying. From that point on, I started hanging out with him and his crew. They would even walk me home as far as they dared, to ensure my safety. One day, several Mexican gang members approached me – seeing this, my newfound guardians stepped in and shielded me. It didn't do me any favors with the Mexican gang, yet the protection I got made me feel safe and provided me with a sense of belonging. Although I wasn't officially part of the gang, they became like a family to me. They saw how I was constantly getting jumped by my people and intervened to protect me. It was a unique bond formed out of necessity and compassion.

As time went on, I found strength in the world of boxing. It became my refuge, my escape from the harsh realities I faced every day. I got pretty good and as a result, the altercations with my father escalated into fistfights, a horrifying reality that no child should ever have to face. Ultimately, that led to my removal from the home. Ironically, being uprooted as a teenager was the best thing that could have happened to me at the time. At sixteen, I found myself in the unfamiliar territory of a foster home. It was the first time I ever felt a semblance of normalcy and family unity, yet the domestic violence I grew up in kept me from fully embracing my new environment. The decision to remove me was a necessary one and came at a heavy price. My father, feeling betrayed by my removal from the home, uttered words that cut deep into my soul. The sincerity in his eyes as he told me "Consider yourself dead to me, and me dead to you," crushed me. Unwilling to show it, I knew our relationship was permanently severed.

A year later, the court decided it was appropriate for me to go back home. Things quickly returned to normal, and I was faced with either moving to Mexico to live on the side of a gym and pursue boxing until I could return to the U.S. as a pro, or I could join the Navy and box as my recruiter told me I could. I chose to join the Navy because I couldn't bear staying at home any longer and the promise of being able to box and get paid a salary was too alluring to pass up – I left and never looked back.

There was a lot of emphasis on bravado, with phrases like 'boys don't cry' and 'suck it up.' Discipline at home was strict and extreme. If I didn't know something my dad would smack me upside the head or yank my ears like a lawnmower pull cable. I vividly remember getting whipped because I tripped and fell on my knee when I was seven years old. My pants were torn and the skin on my knee scraped off and was bleeding. My dad became furious – how dare I tear my pants and get blood on them – and discipline never came with any compassion.

He had this deer foot with strands of leather and polished beads at the end that he would whip my sister and I with when we would get in trouble. I would shield her and take the brunt of the punishment on myself. This kind of torture from my dad was a normal part of growing up. No one thought to call CPS, at least not where I grew up. This kind of upbringing caused a lot of anger and aggression that stayed with me well into my adult years.

I also held resentment towards my mom for many years because she would take my sister and I and leave my dad, only to go back home whenever he found us. When we would leave him, we would stay with church friends in Santa Barbara, San Luis Obispo, and Santa Maria. Somehow, my dad would find us, seem remorseful and apologetic (which I later realized were patterns of an abusive person) and my mom would take him back. He would show up with gifts, take us places that we'd never normally go to and before we knew it, we were on our way back home. Once home, it wasn't long before things went right back to the hell they had always been.

My mother conditioned herself to the life she had to give us the best life that she could. My biological parents are still married and live together to this day, although they don't share the same space. I've asked my mom about her decisions, and she explained that she wanted to provide us stability. She didn't want to worry about where the next meal would come from or if she could make the rent, and instead, chose to endure domestic violence. Looking back, I can understand her perspective, yet as a child, it was a difficult one to comprehend.

As a child, I developed a fear of ignorance because not knowing something would lead to punishment. Even today, I feel uneasy when confronted with unfamiliar topics. I'll spend hours googling whatever it is so I can better understand it and avoid the feeling of not knowing – and that lingering fear of punishment that I had grown to embrace as anger and rage.

I didn't have the best blueprint for fatherhood and vowed not to be like my dad. Over the years I realized that not being my father didn't make me a good father – it only made me "not" him. When I got married and started a family, I realized there were still remnants of my upbringing that I hadn't reconciled with; it would be over a decade before my healing journey began.

I often found myself quick to snap at the children, reprimanding them, taking their toys, embarrassing them in front of their friends, or yelling at them. I was quick to anger and wanted someone to give me a reason to get into an altercation – it was euphoric and made me feel alive. Winning or losing didn't matter as much as releasing the built-up aggression since childhood that had only compounded over the years. I craved conflict, as loud and as intense and violent as possible. Once I became consciously aware of my destructive behaviors, I didn't know how I would overcome them, I just knew I wasn't going to fail at overcoming them.

Decades later, through much reflection and healing, I understood why my dad was the way was. He was repeating what he was conditioned to as a child, raised the same way. Although it was a challenging and demoralizing way to live, I now have empathy and grace for my dad.

I believe God provides opportunities to grow in the areas we desire. I desired to be the best version of myself, and because of my consciousness, I was gifted the opportunity to do better than my father. I desired a career that I was passionate about and I was gifted with the opportunity to first heal my past so that I could discover it. The gifts of being removed from my home, being fired from a position, and seeing my military career derailed, helped redirect my energy towards a new beginning – my life's purpose. I desired patience, and I was gifted with Ryker, my yellow lab service animal. I got him when he was eight weeks old through an organization that trains and certifies dogs as service animals. After twenty-four months of training, it was Ryker who taught me what patience and unconditional love felt like. He has this incredible ability to ground me and help me pause before reacting. Despite his quirks and mischievousness, how could I possibly get mad at him? This helped me realize that if I can extend patience and grace to a dog, I can extend the same patience and grace to people, including myself.

Growing up, my goal was to make it to my 18th birthday alive. I remember having a teddy bear named Tony who I would talk to about what comes after turning eighteen. I would tell Tony that if I ever had a son, I'd name him Zion because it means God's dwelling place. At twenty-three years of age, on February 23rd, 2001, at 7:01 P.M., my wife and I welcomed our first-born son and named him Zion. It was also the last time I quit drinking alcohol, after several failed attempts to stop.

The change we seek lies in the opportunities we are gifted. It is up to us to stretch ourselves and reach for them. Often, it's uncomfortable, yet necessary. It didn't matter where I grew up or whether I was discriminated against by my people because of the color of my skin, or the trauma I survived. What mattered was what I was going to do with it, how I was going to break the cycle and change the narrative of my story. It was up to me to decide - we all have the power to do the same.

Our past doesn't determine our future – it's the journey and the discoveries along the way that help us shape it. By taking the time to understand and connect with others, we discover that our similarities are greater than our differences. When we calm our minds, open our hearts, and establish a profound connection with God, we can surpass the limitations we impose on ourselves and discern the path that has been divinely designed for us. By slowing down, reflecting, and tuning in to our self-energy, we can access the wisdom and guidance already within us. It is in these moments of stillness and receptiveness that we can truly comprehend and embrace our God-given purpose, allowing it to unfold and manifest in our lives.

JOANNE SIRACUSA

Director of Operations,
The MindShift Game

Joanne is a highly experienced educator and administrator who supports growth and development. With a passion for promoting inclusive learning environments as well as personal and professional development. With credentials in Education, Human Resources, and Compliance Administration, she brings a diverse skill set to her work. Joanne has a comprehensive understanding of the educational landscape and is committed to creating a supportive and nurturing atmosphere. Her expertise lies in curriculum creation and designing innovative classes that engage and inspire learners. She is also known for her dedication to mentoring student teachers and providing training and development opportunities to enhance teaching skills.

Peace is Everything

Life unfolds in ways that are meant to shape and empower us. It is through these experiences that we are prepared and equipped for our purpose. God gives us a purpose, a vision, or both, and He strategically places individuals in our lives who will support us in fulfilling it. In scripture, we see that God does not choose those who are already equipped for His divine assignments. Instead, He selects the most unlikely candidates—the broken and the weak. For instance, Joseph was betrayed by his brothers and sold into slavery before ascending to become a powerful ruler. Paul, one of Jesus's disciples, was once a persecutor of Christians before he turned his life around. Moses, too, struggled with insecurities and a speech impediment, yet God called him to confront the mighty Pharaoh and lead the Israelites out of Egypt. Time and time again, the Bible showcases how God chooses individuals seemingly incapable of achieving great things. Similarly, this is the narrative of my life. I was a young girl in a Peruvian-Argentinian family, struggling with my own challenges while also speaking my mind. Looking back, I see that God led me to free myself from my family's generational cycles so He could mold me into who I am today.

"For I know the plans I have for you," declares the Lord, "plans to prosper you and not to harm you, plans to give you hope and a future."
— Jeremiah 29:11

My mother wanted to name me Michelle, however, the day I was born, my father changed it to Joanne. Interestingly, both our names share the same initials, JRS, which is probably why he gave me the name he did. As I grew up, I was closer to my father. This dynamic resulted in me shouldering a greater sense of responsibility. I recently truly grasped the weight and magnitude of this load.

In my household, Spanish was our primary language, and with that came a lot of passionate conversations filled with loud voices, not because we were fighting. It was just how we spoke when talking, casually or passionately. It was common for friends who didn't speak Spanish to mistakenly assume that we were arguing. I got the best of both worlds because, despite my father's strict ways, my mother was more easygoing, so I would frequently go wherever she went. However, living in such an environment meant conforming to certain expectations and behaviors that contradicted my naturally spunky personality. I was rarely told what to do, so I had a lot of independence and often made important decisions on my own. It was instilled in me to not interrupt adult conversations, always greet everyone upon entering a room, and only speak when spoken to. The concept of "what happens here stays here" caused fear of criticism and made me self-conscious. I found it difficult to be vulnerable and discuss anything about my life because I was afraid that oversharing would result in disapproval and criticism.

Throughout my childhood, I repeatedly heard "Uy que van a decir" (What will people say?). This echoed in my mind, and for years, I lived with that constant worry. Fear of other people's opinions and criticism led me to overthink every action, and when I made a mistake, it felt like the end of the world. The burden of shame and guilt was overwhelming. It took time and a shift in my thinking to free myself of those ideas.

It has always struck me as odd when my friends recalled details about their childhood, and I was not able to relate because I had very few memories of mine. Whenever asked to share about my life, I would freeze, unsure of how to respond. How could I skip over my childhood, when it was such a formative period in shaping who I became? Memories of phrases I heard during that time immediately come to mind: "What will people think?" and "What will they say?" created a battle between who I was and my authentic self.

Part of me would think, "Who cares?" and there were certainly moments when I genuinely didn't, yet for the most part, I did. My optimistic side wanted to overlook any unhappy memories. It was a profound realization that not remembering my childhood didn't necessarily mean it was a negative experience. It's fascinating to observe the coping mechanisms we develop, and even more fascinating is the self-awareness that emerges when we embark on a journey of healing. Through introspection, I came to realize that I had subconsciously suppressed memories that didn't bring me peace. Maintaining a sense of tranquility and harmony within myself has always been of utmost importance, and I instinctively shielded myself from disturbances. It made me question the concept of strength and what it truly means. Behind every experience, we tap into greater strength within us, which helps us get through it.

As I go through this process, I recall more childhood memories. I remember going to church every Sunday, our elementary school weekly assemblies, and our principal ending them by saying, "Keep your feet on the ground and reach for the stars." The fun sleepovers at my cousin's house, the trips to Thrifty's for ice cream, and playing Barbies with my sister and giving them questionable makeovers. Memories of roller skating, watching GLOW with my sister, and then dressing up like them and wrestling on my parents' bed. I also realized that there were moments of emotional neglect. I didn't feel comfortable or know how to ask for what I wanted or needed, and I was concerned about depending on others. I can now say, "I need you," which means I trust and want you to help me navigate life. Saying no without feeling guilty was a struggle for me, as I felt responsible for people's happiness. Expressing my feelings and recognizing my strengths were also areas where I faced difficulties, as well as setting boundaries. I've learned that I honor myself when I set boundaries because it allows me to show up for others authentically. Through self-love, I've learned to take care of myself, invest in my personal development, and set healthy boundaries. I now help others without exhausting myself.

As a child, we had parakeets for pets. My father would trim their wings to prevent them from flying too high and getting hurt. I recently realized that, unintentionally, this overprotectiveness also affected us as a family. It instilled in me a tendency to always play it safe and remain in my comfort zone. I was not meant to live in fear and constantly seek safety. I can exercise caution without being overly cautious or careless. Thankfully, God has always placed individuals in my life who have reminded me of my true potential and purpose.

"Perhaps this is the moment for which you have been created."
– Esther 4:14

Behind every strong person lies a story that shapes their strength. Regardless of a person's background or home life, we all possess the choice and power to transform our lives. In my journey, I have come to see my life as a precious gift, and I choose to view every struggle as a valuable lesson. I now recognize that setbacks and rejections are opportunities for growth and development and that my experiences have not defined me; they have instead redefined me. I shape my life through my choices and actions.

Forgiveness has been essential in my evolution; it's important to offer grace to ourselves and others, recognizing that we are all on our own unique journey. I am grateful for the awareness I have gained and the conscious decision I have made to break free from old limiting patterns. It's a process of breaking patterns and finding joy in the present moment. There were times when my life was so busy and fast-paced that I had to intentionally slow down to truly appreciate the blessings that surrounded me. Through this process, I have discovered that vulnerability and strength can coexist, and it is perfectly okay to ask for help. I do not have to carry the weight of the world on my shoulders, and sharing my opinions can be done with love and kindness.

Choosing to heal from old, unconscious family-limiting belief systems has been a transformative experience for me, driven by the understanding that our children deserve the best versions of us. We all possess inherent strength and power within us. Some of us never found the time to be happy because we were too busy being strong. We built walls to protect ourselves, forgetting that these barriers also keep people out. However, through the process of healing, we can break down these walls and embrace the freedom that comes with it. True strength lies within, waiting to be discovered and nurtured. It is through our healing journey that we can unlock our full potential and live a life filled with love, peace, and joy.

In high school, I was presented with a once-in-a-lifetime opportunity to receive a full scholarship, but I decided not to take it. There were two reasons for my decision. First, my family wanted me to stay close, as this opportunity required me to move out of state. Second, I was nervous about the unknown because no one in my immediate family had gone to university. Fighting fear with faith, fear had been an obstacle in my life, preventing me from pursuing many goals. Fear paralyzed me while faith propelled me. Through investing in my personal growth and engaging in self-reflection, I have gained valuable insights about why I do what I do.

This unexpected turn of events led me to pursue a career in education. It was a transformative experience because the teacher of my first class was the director of the preschool at the College Child Development Center. She was impressed with my commitment in the classroom and asked me to bring her my resume. I thought she would help me improve it, and to my surprise, she offered me a job. During my time at the community college, I also worked as a student mentor, assisting other student teachers on their academic journey.

I believe I was drawn to the field of education and working with children because it allowed me to tap into my inner child and let her shine again. I started my journey by going to school and pursuing a career in education. I dedicated a good fifteen years of my life to this field. I truly enjoyed working in education and was very fulfilled, especially being a Regional Director at the YMCA because the nonprofit sector is aligned with my values. In this role, I hired, trained, licensed, and created enrichment programs, and managed operations across the Western Region. Then one day, while I was praying, I felt the nudge that it was time to make a significant change in my career, and it became very clear that a change was necessary in my life. To explore my options, I decided to take a human resources class at a local college. I wanted to see if pursuing a degree in Business Administration or something similar would be a good fit for me. Coincidentally, the class I took aligned perfectly with my role at the YMCA, as I had already been involved in the hiring process and administrative tasks. This led me to discover a newfound passion for Human Resources, specifically in the field of Training and Development.

The first opportunity that presented itself was in an administrative role at an international construction company. Intrigued, I decided to explore this opportunity in the private sector, and that's how I found myself in the construction world! My role encompasses various aspects, such as assisting in the Diversity Department, which I absolutely love. This is what drew me to education, which I also started in an administrative role. I thought that this was a good way to ease into the company and gain some experience outside of my education background. I had a strategic plan in mind, thinking I would stay for a year or two, five at most, and then reassess my options. After one year, I realized that I needed a new challenge. I spoke with my supervisor and expressed my interest in the Diversity Department, and he agreed to let me explore it. The diversity manager was excited for me to come into her department and support her. It was a new department at that time. This allowed me to grow my diversity knowledge, learn, and help Small Businesses and DBEs (disadvantaged businesses), which include Minority, Women-Owned, and veteran-owned businesses. Connecting with people and making a difference is what I believe my purpose in life is.

"Be transformed by the renewing of your mind." – Romans 12:2

I began my healing journey with Rocío Pérez a few years ago. With her support, I uncovered the importance of healthy boundaries. This awareness has brought me a sense of freedom. When Rocío approached me about running a pilot for *The MindShift Game,* I immediately joined her in this endeavor. The game aligns perfectly with my passion for being of service and supporting others on their own journeys. It allows me to make a positive impact in people's lives. I believe in the power of *The MindShift Game* and its ability to help individuals embrace their true potential. It encompasses affirmations, helps us visualize our future, take bold actions toward our goals, and solidify our belief in what is possible for ourselves. The game encourages gratitude, which has been proven to have numerous health benefits. It resonates with every aspect of my life, as I am constantly learning and growing. Above all, I cherish the genuine connections I can make with others. I have the privilege of walking alongside people dedicated to healing, transformation, and personal development.

I am now the Director of Operations for *The MindShift Game.* During our daily calls, we often talk about freedom of expression and how it supports us in becoming a better version of ourselves. When we hold back and suppress our thoughts and feelings, it only builds up and makes us more reactive and resentful. Yet when we speak freely, it brings a sense of release and allows us to connect with others on a deeper level and in a safe space.

"The pain that you're feeling, can't compare to the joy that's coming."
– Romans 8:18

Everyone faces challenges in life, and it is through these challenges that we can grow. Change is a gradual process that becomes ingrained in our daily lives. I believe there is power in perseverance, purpose in pain, growth in the process, and beauty in the journey.

The key is giving what we wish we would have received. It's important to be the kind of adult children need and extend that support to others. This is what makes the difference. Building community and surrounding ourselves with like-minded individuals is essential. Finding people who align with our values and goals may not always be easy, and having even one person in our corner can make a world of difference. Over time, we can develop the ability to open ourselves up to others and form deep connections. These relationships have the power to reshape our lives and guide us to a better version of ourselves.

"Two people are better off than one, for they can help each other succeed."
– Ecclesiastes 4:9

Being intentional about who you keep in your life will help you succeed. Sometimes, progress is not possible until you have changed your circle. Not to be alone, because isolation, or loneliness, is a disadvantage in times of difficulty, but change your circle by surrounding yourself with new people that will elevate you. Often, this is the key to success. The people we choose to surround ourselves with have a tremendous influence on our lives. At my core, I choose to embrace joy and peace. As it is written in Psalm 29:11, "The Lord gives his people strength, and the Lord blesses his people with peace."

I am filled with gratitude for the people who entered my life and brought out the best in me. They saw the beauty within me when I couldn't see it myself. It is important to share with others the positive qualities we see in them. You never know how it may shape their path. Doing this creates a synergy between you and the people in your life, which in turn is how strong support systems that foster community are created, which leads to incredible opportunities.

The journey of transcending my inherited limitations and attaining true liberation has been an extraordinary adventure. I feel exhilaration akin to a child in a candy store as if I possess a secret that everyone needs to know. This is what drives me to reach out to others and share my knowledge. One of the most profound lessons I have learned is the importance of releasing and letting go. Letting go of the past, the pain, the suffering, and the mistakes. Although it is not an easy task, it is a crucial step towards personal growth and moving forward. Additionally, when it comes to expressing gratitude, I am overwhelmed with appreciation for my past experiences. Without them, I would not be where I am today. I want to express my heartfelt gratitude to God for His unwavering presence in my life and for all that He has accomplished, is currently accomplishing, and will continue to accomplish. I am also deeply grateful to my father for ensuring my safety, my mother for introducing me to the core principles of my faith, my sister for the countless moments of laughter and thrilling adventures, and my friends who have become my chosen family and supported me through every season of life. Even those individuals who were only present in my life for a brief period, I extend my gratitude to them for the valuable lessons they imparted. As I embark on this ongoing journey, I am filled with anticipation for the future and eager to witness the path that God will guide me towards.

Our greatest accomplishment is really who you were as a person. It's really about the legacy you leave behind.

PAM COVARRUBIAS

Producer and Host,
Café con Pam

Pam Covarrubias became the coach her immigrant mom needed. Pam is a Coach, Speaker, Podcaster, and Recovering Procrastinator.

Grounded in liberation principles, she employs trauma-informed practices that nurture her clients' nervous systems. Rejecting the damages of Calladita Culture™, Pam embraces her voice to eradicate its impact by advocating against silencing and submission in first-generation women and femmes in the U.S.

As the host of the globally acclaimed podcast, Cafe con Pam, she shares candid, thought-provoking insights from diverse voices, offering a valuable resource for those seeking business success and community-driven positive change.

The Choices in Our Story

Deep within my spirit is a little girl. She was quiet for a long time but not anymore. I had forgotten about her for a while because I didn't understand how she was so forgiving, so loving, so free, and full of life, my focus was solely on the external circumstances surrounding me. As life unfolded, as it tends to do, I had no choice but to turn to the little girl for answers. We embraced and she taught me how to set down my anger and resentment so that I could forgive and let go, how to live free of all the burdens of the past, and how to laugh and have fun even in the dark. She's been here showing me that I am not alone, and the possibilities for my future are endless. Since then, my life has never been the same.

Ever since I turned to the inner child within me for guidance, I have come to realize that everyone can connect and nurture their own inner child, and because of society's expectations, many of us have somehow forgotten about our younger selves. We have buried our innocent, loving nature and traded it for the cold indifference that the world offers. In the process, we slowly lose touch with who we once were and the dreams that used to ignite our souls. We push away any thoughts or memories that resurface to remind us, and we suppress our spirit from trying to awaken us. However, this transformation does not occur on its own. Something triggers it, something so traumatic that it brings tears to our eyes when we reflect on it in solitude. For me, that event was when my father abandoned our family when I was eleven years old. I was devastated and utterly confused because, until that point, I had been a daddy's girl.

I was an only child until I turned six years old. Being the sole focus of my parents' attention had its perks, but deep down, I longed for a companion, a little sister to share my childhood adventures with. From the age of two, I began writing heartfelt letters to the stork, hoping that my wishes would come true. My mother's struggle with fertility issues added a layer of complexity to my yearning for a sibling. It pained her to see me yearn for a sister, knowing that her own body was unable to fulfill that desire. Every day, without fail, I would pen a letter to the stork, asking when it would bring me a little sister. I would carefully tuck the letters under the front door, a comical attempt to send them outside in hopes the stork could pick them up. As my mother left for work each day, she would discover my letters and undoubtedly shed tears of both joy and sadness. She had exhausted every available option and six long years passed, filled with hope, disappointment, and unwavering determination. Then, finally, after years of waiting, The Universe answered my letters, and my sister was born. Her arrival brought immeasurable happiness to our family. The void that had lingered for so long was finally filled, and I reveled in the newfound bond with my little sister. I didn't think it could get better, and then only one year later, my brother joined our family, completing the trio of siblings. Our household was now filled with laughter, chaos, and an abundance of love, or, so, that's what I had thought.

Four years later, all our lives were turned upside down. My mom took us kids on a vacation, and we returned home to our father gone. All that was left was a letter to us. Although I was devastated, I was also torn between devastation and relief. My father was an alcoholic, and for as long as I could remember, his alcoholism had been an issue in the house.

In the wake of this loss, my mother found herself thrust into the role of a single parent and could no longer leave us three children to go to work. With three children to provide and care for, the weight of responsibility fell squarely on her shoulders. It was a daunting task, one that would have broken many, but my mother's resilience and determination shone through. Instead of succumbing to despair, my mother tapped into her resourcefulness and embarked on a journey of self-reliance. The first year or so was the most difficult, especially around Father's Day and other celebrations and watching other children have their father with them. My mom would see the disappointment and sadness across my face and would quickly remind me of the one message she always reinforced to me growing up- the power of choice. She emphasized that while we cannot control what others say or do, we can choose how we respond. This empowering perspective allowed me to understand that I always had a choice in how I navigated these situations. Whether it was standing in my own power, ignoring negativity, or responding in a way that would bring about positive outcomes, the choice was mine to make. My mother's guidance taught me the importance of considering my options and making thoughtful choices before taking any action. This message became part of my foundation as an adult and is what I would remember when faced with difficult circumstances.

My mother was determined to create a stable and secure future for us children, so she started her own business from her crafting hobby. It was in this single-mother household that I grew up in, witnessing firsthand the strength and resilience that can be found in the face of adversity. She began by creating ceramic figures using a specific dry brushing technique, which she then found her signature style. The demand for her creations grew fast, leading her to establish her own factory. It soon became a thriving operation, and instead of hiring people from the outside to help, she hired her family members because she wanted to bring everyone up with her. However, the loyalty my mom had was definitely not reciprocated, and when she realized her own family had been stealing from her, she lost her entire business because of it. Regardless of how her business ended, watching my mom work so hard day and night to provide for us, and create a thriving business by herself out of a simple hobby was absolutely remarkable and inspiring.

Once again, my mother was not only betrayed but also found herself under extreme financial strain. She decided to move all of us back to the States to live with her cousin because she was understandably at odds with her family in Mexico. In one of my ESL classes, I formed a close friendship with a Brazilian girl who spoke Portuguese, and we discovered that we could communicate effectively due to the similarities between our languages. However, we both agreed we had an immense desire to learn English. I made the decision to fully immerse myself in the language. During one summer, my mother insisted I go visit my father and spend the summer with him. However, when it was time for me to return to school, I was surprised by the news that I would be staying with my father in Mexico. Initially, I harbored resentment towards my father for leaving us.

Living with Dad for the next few years proved to be a healing experience. My father's strong spiritual beliefs and our deep conversations opened my eyes to the power of forgiveness. Through these discussions, I began to understand that holding onto resentment and anger only hindered my own growth and happiness. I learned that there was more to our souls than the temporary emotions and conflicts we experience. We had numerous heartfelt conversations, and he had the opportunity to explain himself to me. I didn't fully agree with his choices, but my mother's words echoed in my mind, that I had the power to make a choice. In that moment, I decided to see the human in my father, and accept him for who he was. This moment also gave life to me, and our love was bigger than the hurt and mistakes. After I made the decision not to carry the baggage of resentment and anger with me, I was free to love my father for who he was. I had to love myself enough to let go so that I would be liberated from the heaviness of anger. Up to that point, my self-talk was filled with loathing and hate for myself. I would often tell myself that I didn't even deserve a dad, so why did I deserve anything else? After I freed myself up from carrying the weight of anger and resentment, the way I started speaking to myself also changed.

As a U.S. citizen, I embraced the opportunity to expand my horizons by attending college in Missouri, marking the beginning of my journey as a "backwards immigrant." Being a city girl all my life, I figured I could use an adventure and experience a different scenery, so I packed my bags at nineteen years old and headed to the Midwest.

The experience of struggling to fit my complex identity into pre-defined boxes spurred a profound exploration of my evolving sense of self. Battling ADHD, depression, and anxiety along the way, I delved deep into understanding my unique brain wiring and how to nurture my well-being. This led me to a profound exploration of my own identity. In Missouri, the scarcity of diversity compelled me to delve deep into my sense of self to truly understand who I was, as there was no one else like me to serve as a reference point. I found solace in reflecting upon moments when I was not confined to societal expectations, allowing me to rediscover and embrace my true essence. Rejecting medication, I opted for a more holistic approach centered around self-care practices like journaling, whole food consumption, and mindfulness meditation. I also discovered the transformative power of Emotional Freedom Techniques (EFT) or tapping for nervous system regulation, a crucial step in coping with challenges while making thoughtful choices.

Taking tests and sitting through long lectures was never my strong point. I wanted to understand why my brain was "broken" and discovered I had ADHD, which led to depression and anxiety. During a design project, my professor pointed out my procrastination and self-sabotage. This moment made me, once again, remember my mother's words about choices, and I started to reflect on the choices I was making and how they were impacting my path. Through EFT, I learned the importance of regulating the nervous system before making decisions. Tapping helps achieve nervous system regulation and clarity by balancing the amygdala, our brain's alarm system.

This practice has not only helped me personally but has also become an integral part of the work I do with others as a Certified Clinical EFT Practitioner. By embracing nervous system regulation techniques like tapping and educating myself about the intricacies of ADHD, I have been able to navigate my own unique challenges and find a path toward self-acceptance and growth. I now view it as my superpower and use it to my advantage in all areas of my life.

I learned from my father about the power of the mind. For over ten years, I have been practicing as an EFT practitioner and coach, supporting nervous system regulation and identity exploration in first-generation individuals in the U.S. I have also deepened my knowledge of trauma and mental health, witnessing the transformative power of Emotional Freedom Techniques. Through EFT, I have gained a profound understanding of how trauma is stored in the body. Our bodies bear the burdens of unresolved painful events and chronic stress.

The body's innate healing wisdom is truly amazing once we create the right conditions. Through EFT, I have seen incredible results with clients, affirming that the body knows the way back to wholeness. My passion is helping people tune into their body's self-healing abilities and release what weighs them down, so they can find inner peace and hope. This work has a ripple effect, uplifting communities and societies.

During my exploration of self, podcasts that resonated with my experiences helped me. I desired to hear others' stories through interviews, feeling connected to them on a deeper level. Despite struggling to find such podcasts initially, I remained determined and waited for three years before taking matters into my own hands. In 2016, I bought a microphone from Craigslist, marking the beginning of my podcasting journey. Since then, my podcast, Café con Pam, has gained global recognition, being streamed in over forty countries. It has played a significant role in my healing journey and continues to push me to grow in each stage of my life.

My trailblazing podcast examining bilingual mental health from personal and professional perspectives became the only one of its kind for several years thereafter. Café con Pam is now recognized as a pioneering voice expanding diverse representation in podcasting and it has catapulted far beyond a passion project into a source of purpose, healing, and growth.

At each transitional juncture for me, my show has stretched to encompass broader dimensions too. Through unrelenting highs and lows, my show has shouldered sacred witness to the unpacking of old wounds and the alchemy of their transformation into wisdom earned and lessons for others. It carries my hope that anyone feeling unseen or voiceless may know that their unique light deserves to be known and held with gentle compassion. My dream now is that the ripples of Café con Pam will continue empowering people across borders and identities to rewrite their destinies from places of courage and self-love.

During my journey of self-discovery and entrepreneurship, I realized the importance of investing in myself. I decided to hire a business coach who helped me grow my business. As we worked together, my coach pointed out that I was actually doing more than just creative directing. I was coaching my clients, strategizing, and helping them create better brands. After some internal struggle, I finally embraced the idea of being a business coach. I obtained my EFT training and life coaching certification and started offering both branding and coaching services. Eventually, I decided to focus solely on coaching and closed the branding aspect of my business. Throughout this journey, my podcast has remained a consistent part of my life and continues to thrive.

The thousands of tiny choices that make up my path so far have led me here, to this current moment of contemplation about the origins of my identity. And though the road of trials and triumphs stretches far behind me, I can see now that within me lives the wisdom and resilience of all my prior selves - those I have given voice to through stories, and those yet unrealized. My life until now has been but a preview of the wonders yet to come. And so, taking a deep breath to center myself in the vast realm of possibility, I open my heart and take the next step with my listeners and clients walking alongside, together.

MAVI BARRAZA

Author | Speaker | Journalist

Mavi is a trailblazer, an inspiring entrepreneur, and a remarkable communicator. With almost three decades of experience in local media and Spanish-language press, Mavi has continuously pushed boundaries and developed groundbreaking communication strategies and marketing campaigns. Her profound understanding of the Hispanic community in Colorado and unwavering passion for progressive causes have made her a powerful advocate and voice for the Latino community. Mavi's dedication to inclusivity and her ability to connect with people on a deep level make her a true force for positive change. She is an inspiration to all who aspire to make a difference in the world.

My Story in The Country of ... Opportunities?

My parents immigrated to "El Norte," the United States without their children in search of a better life. In 1991, while I was in Mexico and the United States fought in the Cold War, my parents made a life-changing decision, a choice that would impact my life and wreak havoc on it like the war itself. Two years after their departure, my mom returned to Mexico to take me and my siblings to the land of opportunities.

In the 1980's, my father was a manager at Conasupo warehouses, a popular state-owned company that subsidized products to help the neediest people in urban and rural areas. He tried his luck as an entrepreneur and became the owner of a sawmill which provided jobs to many people in low-income neighborhoods. The company was doing well or so we thought, until one day the "Federales," the federal government, appeared at our home looking for my dad. My father received a lawsuit from "Hacienda," the Mexican IRS, because of his accountant's illegal actions and fled the country to avoid legal repercussions. My mother left for the U.S. a year later. At that moment, the final chapter of my life in the land of my birth began.

I was the firstborn and the first granddaughter and niece on my father's side, this played a central role in shaping my upbringing. When I was born, my grandmother, a single mother of three children and the midwife of the town decided she would raise me as her daughter. I am proud to be "criada por mi abuela," raised by my grandmother *(Ama)*; she shaped my personality and positively impacted my life.

I was eleven years old, savoring my childhood in the late summer of 1991 when my biological mother returned home after a year in the U.S. I was happily playing with my ball when she called to instruct me to pack my bags as we would be leaving for Colorado in three days. This felt like a death sentence.

"What? But why?" I asked without getting an answer. Unfortunately, my pleas didn't change my parents' decision. What would happen to my *Ama?* I wondered if she would come with us or be completely alone if she stayed. We left her behind.

The End of The World (My World) and The Beginning of My New Reality

As I sat on the window seat of the bus that took us to the border, my *Ama* leaned against the huge window overlooking the bus terminal; I helplessly watched my heartbroken Abuelita sink down onto the floor as our bus moved past her slowly. She was devastated. Her reason for existing was leaving on that bus–her daughter and grandchildren.

Our Abuelita lived for us. About two years earlier, she had been diagnosed with breast cancer. She was caring for us at the time and drew the strength to endure the grueling chemotherapy and radiation treatments, which I accompanied her to. In that precise moment, I learned what soul-piercing pain was, seeing the pillar of my life, the matriarch of my family, the strength of an entire town crumble to the ground in front of me. I felt that way for many, many years, as if my soul had been shattered by so much pain.

After a twelve-hour journey, we entered the States with a tourist visa. I knew I was *en el otro lado* (the U.S.) when we stopped at McDonald's to eat; the restaurant had a very peculiar and amusing look. My mother suggested I order a hamburger. I laughed when I saw it as I had never seen such a small and plain hamburger.

I remember asking jokingly: What is this? Anyone who has had Mexican hamburgers will know what I mean. That was my first unsavory welcome to the *gabacho,* the "U.S."

That was the beginning of my great disappointment with the neighboring country. After another twelve hours, we arrived in Denver after dark. As we passed Santa Fe District, my mom shared excitedly "Look, your cousin lives in that apartment building." I exclaimed with surprise, "Here?" I had never seen anything like it. It was a run-down white building.

My uncle, who had accompanied my dad to pick us up at the border, was driving; he looked in the rearview mirror and said, "Oh! Wait until you see where you're going to live." Soon we arrived at our apartment; it was dirty, smelly, and full of cockroaches. It had one tiny bedroom which only fit a twin-sized bed for my two siblings, my parents and me. My uncle and his then-wife slept on a sofa bed in the dining/living room. They decided to move to Colorado to live with my parents a few months before we arrived.

To my young eyes, all the adults in the house worked odd jobs. My aunt had studied to be a bilingual receptionist, and here, she worked in a fast-food restaurant. My uncle, a food engineer, worked in construction. My dad went from being a small business owner of a wooden gate factory to being a dishwasher at a restaurant. And my mother, who owned and operated her own grocery store in the city back home, now worked the night-shift cleaning offices in corporate America.

My siblings were enrolled in school a few days after our arrival in this country; however, things were different for me. I spent most of my days locked in the apartment, crying, and feeling miserable. My father changed after living in the U.S. for two years. He refused to let me attend school, saying that girls didn't need education and should work instead. He planned to buy forged documents for me to start working.

After a short time, we moved into a bigger house yet continued to live in poverty and lacked our basic necessities. Once, we had to eat potato chip sandwiches and Oreo cookies. My parents found the chips near the trash can in the offices my mom cleaned, and my mom bought sandwich bread from the local 7-Eleven. I remember my three-year-old sister crying and vomiting from hunger. I found fruit in the pantry and gave her a piece. When my aunt caught me in the kitchen, she warned me not to take her food again. I didn't say anything in response.

My father had changed so much. He had lost everything and had to start from scratch in a new country with a new language he did not speak, where his business skills and experience were obsolete. It must have all been very difficult for him. When we lived in Mexico, he was a businessman who carried a briefcase, drove a nice car, and dressed formally; he listened to Mozart and Beethoven's music and read and wrote poetry—that's how I remember him. In the U.S., he was unrecognizable. His ideas had changed for the worse. He started partying with undesirable people and began drinking alcohol, and over time his temperament became very aggressive.

One November afternoon, my mom sent me to a friend's house to pick up food. She lived a couple blocks away on the second floor of our old apartment complex. It was days before I saw my mom again. I was kidnapped. Twenty-four hours after I left my home, my photograph and pertinent details were widely shared through various media channels. Missing child posters were attached to light poles in the neighborhood, asking: "Have you seen her?" It took police officers three days to find me inside a closet of one of the apartments in the complex. My kidnapper was one of my father's drinking buddies.

When I was finally found, nobody made any attempts to listen to me. They asked no questions. I did not speak or understand English. They simply removed me from my kidnapper's closet, handcuffed me and took me to the police station. I was placed in a shelter for "protection," although I did not understand from what. Without translators, they gestured for me to wash my face in the restroom. Then they transferred me to a shelter for teen girls where I was bullied by delinquent and troubled girls. When I returned home, things around me went back to normal and that chapter of my life was never discussed again.

That unspoken incident added to my state of mourning and depression and staying home from school did not help. My mom took English classes at the school my siblings attended and one day she took me with her. During class, the English teacher discovered that my father had forbidden me from attending school. Days later, my parents received a letter informing them that keeping me home from school was against the law. I was finally able to go to school.

To make matters worse, in mid-April of 1992, my parents received a call informing us that my grandmother, my caretaker, the woman who had raised me, was in her last days. If we wanted to see her alive, we had to return to Durango immediately. My mom received help from a psychologist she had recently met, someone who knew what I had been through. This kind woman gave my mom $300 in cash and instructed her, "Take this girl to see her mom *(Ama)*." I returned to my beloved hometown seven months after leaving, in time to share a few precious minutes with my *Ama*, the most significant person in my life, before she passed.

When my Abuelita died, I felt like an abandoned puppy in the middle of the desert—for many years my body was present while my mind drifted. We returned to the U.S.; I graduated middle school and started high school. The following summer, I worked at a fast-food restaurant. After working three consecutive shifts without calling home, my mom warned me not to come home as my father was infuriated. I slept in a friend's car for a few days.

At fifteen, I moved in with my friend and at sixteen, we got pregnant. That was the end of my time in high school. No longer living with my dad, there was nothing to stop me from pursuing my dream of a higher education, or so I thought. At seventeen, after receiving my GED with much excitement, I enrolled in college, only to leave soon after because I could not afford it.

My Passion for Media and
The Ghost of Immigration

In 1998, my life changed when I discovered an amazing opportunity. I loved listening to the local radio, and a popular Spanish station was searching for talented individuals interested in venturing into media. After auditioning, I was selected out of nearly 100 applicants to receive training and work at the station. I had my first experience with radio four years earlier during the summer when I asked for and was granted the opportunity to be trained as an announcer at a radio station. My mother was my accomplice, seeing the spark in my eyes amidst the sadness of my kidnapping and my grandmother's passing. She secretly took me to practice at the radio station for months. From my first time behind a microphone, I knew I had found my calling in media; that's what I wanted to do for the rest of my life.

During my work at the station, I hosted an early morning music program on weekends and later, worked as a traffic reporter during peak hours. Unfortunately, I had to resign due to workplace conflicts and joined another popular Spanish radio station. I was in my new role a short time before my former bosses informed my new boss about my immigration status–I was not authorized to work in the U.S. legally–leading to my immediate termination. It was then that I decided to pursue my dream of a professional career once more and enrolled in college to earn my degree. However, I had to cut my studies short due to a law that prohibited undocumented students from attending university.

I eventually found myself working at an advertising agency, where I had the chance to showcase my talents as an on-camera personality. This opportunity helped me gain recognition and become one of the official Spanish voices for the Census 2000 campaign in four states. I also had the privilege of being the voice in hundreds of commercials, while also serving as a production assistant for a film. Thanks to my experience at the agency, I was later offered a higher position as an assistant program director at a radio station outside Denver. It was both challenging and incredibly rewarding.

After returning to Denver, I dedicated myself to supporting non-profit organizations focused on teenagers' and children's personal development. Through one of these organizations, I coordinated the first massive soccer match in Denver; it was well-attended and that's where I met my husband. From 2003 to the end of 2005, I focused on my family. In 2006, I returned to radio, this time to a news format. I began as a traffic reporter and eventually became the host, taking charge of the production of the station's flagship program.

In 2008, as the station had reached the pinnacle of its success and popularity, the ghost of immigration returned. The immigration department was alerted to the presence of undocumented individuals working at the station and unfortunately, I had to leave another job I loved.

I was determined to do what it took. My grandmother's *Fortaleza* had inspired me to keep pushing forward, and I didn't want to disappoint my mother, who had always been there for me. Suddenly, I received an email from a contact I had made at the radio station. They informed me about a university that accepted undocumented students and offered a $3,000 scholarship for those who wanted to enroll. With this opportunity in mind, I decided to resume my studies, even though it meant, once more, starting from the beginning.

I had escaped being picked up by the *migra* (immigration) three times by now, and like we say in my *country,* there's no deadline that doesn't get met, and no time that doesn't arrive. In March 2011, I was arrested by the Aurora Police Department after calling 911 for what ended up being a panic attack caused by medication. I was unfairly arrested and spent three days in jail for no reason, with the excuse that "my file was lost." I was then transferred to an immigration detention center.

Usually, detainees are released or deported within a week. I was unfairly detained for three weeks before seeing an immigration judge. It took the intervention from the Consulate General of Mexico for the immigration detention center case manager to realize my file had been misplaced.

I spent a month in agony, unfairly locked up with no contact with my daughters. After being released from the detention center, I began my immigration process again. Surprisingly, immigration had no record of my previous application or any of my past interactions with them, including my entry into the United States, tourist visa, passport, or the recent petition I had submitted. It was as if all evidence of my previous history with immigration had disappeared.

My upcoming immigration court hearing motivated me to finish my Bachelor's in International Business in just two years. This achievement not only demonstrated my commitment to being a responsible citizen and fulfilled my childhood dream. My immigration nightmare continued as my hearing was repeatedly postponed for seven years for various reasons, causing my frustration with this country to grow. From being kidnapped as a pre-teen to being unjustly detained by immigration for a month as an adult, I constantly questioned why I received such treatment.

Since coming to this country, I have accomplished a lot. I started a TV campaign to raise awareness about the dangers of drugs among young people. During the only year I attended high school, I filmed a short infomercial in my art class. As a pioneer I addressed immigration issues and led over 50,000 participants in *Un Día Sin Imigrantes,* a powerful immigration march movement. I provided community assistance through my radio shows to thousands of listeners daily and founded a support group which helped hundreds of women over thirteen years. Additionally, I supported numerous non-profit organizations through personal development workshops and fundraising efforts. I served as the Vice President of the student government at my university for two years and worked as a bilingual communication specialist for the Archdiocese of Denver. My journalistic work has even been recognized by the Catholic Press Association of the United States and Canada.

In 2018, I began working on a plan to return to Mexico or to migrate to another country. I was tired of struggling with the system and the consequences that it had brought to my family. The health of one of my daughters was severely affected, to the point of causing psychological damage that would later manifest in her physical health—all because of her mother's immigration detention. It was during that year that, overnight, I was granted permanent residency.

As you can see, I didn't immigrate to this country as many have, seeking a better life; no, that was not my case. I was brought here without my consent and practically by force. I lost a lot by coming here—the love and care of my grandmother, *Ama,* my friends, my freedom, my happiness, and my entire world. To make things worse, my welcome to this country was catastrophic, and my experience with the legal system and immigration was horrible. Nevertheless, following the example of the two most important women in my life, my biological mother, and my *Ama,* I forged ahead against all odds.

To this day, I have achieved numerous goals, as a mother, an entre-preneur, an author, a motivator, and an athlete. As I write this story, I am taking the final class in my Masters of Science in Organiza-tional Leadership Degree while caring for, raising, and guiding my three daughters, instilling in them values and love for their roots and culture, while maintaining respect for the country where they were born.

I am now living a brand-new chapter in my life as a widow and res-ident of Parker, Colorado. Yes, my soul was shattered once again, and yes, I'm going to continue until I can, despite it all; in memory of my *Ama*, out of respect for my mother and her effort to sup-port me, for my daughters so they have a role model to follow, and because I owe it to myself and my *Fortaleza*.

REPRESENTATION & GENDER EQUITY

VERONICA LAWRENCE ORTEGA

Industrial and Organizational Psychologist

A retired Navy Master Chief, Veronica completed a 24-year career as the Navy's premier subject matter expert on culture, diversity, equity, and inclusion serving as the senior assessor in the Office of the Naval Inspector General. Her undergraduate degree is in Technical Management with a specialization in Criminal Justice, and a graduate degree in Industrial and Organizational Psychology (IOP) and is also a Certified Diversity Professional (CDP). She graduated as a "distinguished graduate" of the Defense Culture Institute and is currently pursuing a doctoral degree in Organizational Change and Leadership at the University of Southern California's Rossier School of Education.

Courage is Speaking Up

I grew up in the heart of the Dominican Republic, in a world of incongruent and opposing love and abuse, where survival and living were the same. Everything started when I was adopted by my then sixty-seven-year-old dad and forty-five-year-old mother. At the time, I was their only child, considering that my parents had children from previous marriages who were thirty years older than me. Why adopt a child at such a late stage in their lives? My mother always longed for a deeper connection with my dad, one she could not forge without a catalyst. Adopting me was the perfect opening for my mother to stay with my dad. Sometimes, being with someone has little to do with love. You see, my dad owned land inherited from his father. He also built and owned the house we lived in. Our house was more like a shack that had dirt floors and only three rooms: the kitchen, the bathroom you showered in, and the living room. The outhouse was in the back of our house, and our showers were essentially us pouring water over ourselves with a cup. There were all kinds of bugs everywhere. It wasn't uncommon to shake off scorpions and tarantulas from my clothes in the morning or have several bug bites all over my body. That was a regular part of my life. Yes, the house was humble and poor, but it was ours and it was home to me.

Still, can a house be a home without love? Dad loved me, and as a result of that, my mother was jealous. She hated me because of my close relationship with him, and it manifested in cruel and abusive behavior towards me while he was at work. This maltreatment only got worse over time. The beatings were a regular, daily part of my life. I never told my dad anything because he worked so long that he was never there to protect me. I didn't think he could. When I was ten, my mother admitted that she only agreed to adopt me to have access to my dad's house if he were to die. She recognized that he was twenty-two years older than her, and it was more likely that he'd pass before her, and without a child, she wouldn't have rights to his house. This assured her she would have a place to live if he died.

Most of my memories of my mom are unpleasant. One day, my mom and I sat in our small, dimly lit living room. I was thirteen-years old, and I'll never forget her emotionless expression, her eyes filled with bitterness and disappointment. She looked at me coldly and said, "A man will never love you. Men will only use you for intercourse. You'll be nothing more than an object to them. Do you hear me?" Her voice dripped with anger. She constantly reminded me how much she hated my hair and commented about how wide my nose was. She called my nose my biggest defect. Those words stayed in my head for years. Over time, it got to me, and I despised my reflection. She had planted seeds that rooted themselves deep in my mind. Yet, the cruelty didn't stop there. My mother would tell me that my obsession with school resulted from my biological family's mental illnesses. She claimed that I, too, had a mental illness and that my dedication to my studies was merely a symptom of my supposed condition. It was as if she was trying to strip away any sense of hope. I never knew what was going to trigger her. As an adult, I now realize that my mother's words reflected her insecurities and unhealed trauma. She gave birth to a baby at fourteen, who ended up dying in her arms. The father of that child left her. She had another child at fifteen. This man also left her. As a single mother, she moved in with my dad when she was twenty-two. She had brothers and sisters but was never close to them. I suspect she never experienced a dad-daughter relationship, and having been rejected by men her entire life, my relationship with my dad directly conflicted with her life's experiences and expectations. My mother's experiences were a breeding ground for anger and resentment, resulting in abuse. Looking at the whole situation through the lens of time and wisdom, I find it sad that she lived her entire life this way. Yet many of us continue that cycle, never fully understanding the root of our anger and unhappiness.

Despite the hardships, I found solace in school, where I could get a short break from my mother's wrath. I'll never forget my third-grade teacher, Ms. Milagros, which in Spanish means miracle. She told me that I was the most intelligent little girl she had ever met and that one statement boosted my confidence so much that I never forgot it- not even after all these years. I believed her, and I allowed my imagination to stretch and to dream of being something I didn't see anyone else doing around me; I dreamt of being a scientist and had this vision of holding a magnifying glass and investigating things. Oddly enough, in some ways, that is close to what I do today.

In 1990, my dad left my mother and married the mother of his biological children. During this time, my mother clung to me to control him. My dad leaving my mother and marrying another woman scared me because his departure left me to live alone with her for the next three years. This was a terrifying time in my life. I was all alone with a woman whose anger was out of control. Surprisingly, she clung to me dearly because I was all she had. For three years, I feared my mother's presence, and she feared my absence. I found peace when my dad told me I was moving with him to the United States. However, my mother cried bitterly when she found out. I was excited to leave the small village I grew up in. Moving to the United States felt like a dream, and I knew it meant I could have a different life than the one I knew. I knew it also meant no more beatings. It was a fresh start, a new beginning, and most importantly, I would be with my dad. It was freedom. Sadly, my mother passed away three years after I left.

Attending my junior year of high school in the United States with limited knowledge of the English language was a daunting experience, but little did I know that fate had something extraordinary in store for me. My ESL teacher, Maria Cunningham, quickly became my guiding light in this new and unfamiliar world. She genuinely liked me and went above and beyond to support me in my journey. She noticed my struggles with reading and immediately acted. Without hesitation, she spent $114 on glasses for me, ensuring I could read and learn more effectively. It was a small gesture that meant the world to me. Her kindness continued. She recognized my potential and believed in me. The Princeton University recruiters visited my school and invited me to their open house event. Ms. Cunningham opened a world of possibilities that I never thought possible. She took me to "meet and greets" for admission and other National Society academic events. Ms. Cunningham believed in me. The fact is that not everyone shared that mindset about me. One day, my history teacher made a hurtful comment, suggesting that I should attend a college that spoke Spanish because I had an accent. I was disheartened and unsure of how to respond. Ms. Cunningham was my advocate and refused to let this injustice go unnoticed. Without a second thought, Ms. Cunningham stormed into the classroom, slamming the door behind her. I couldn't hear the conversation, but I knew Ms. Cunningham had my back. In that moment, I realized the power of having someone in your corner who believes in you when the world seems against you. Ms. Cunningham's support and fierce determination gave me the strength to persevere and prove that I could achieve greatness despite the obstacles. Through all this, I also realized the importance of having someone speak out when injustice is being served.

As a senior in high school, I worked at McDonald's full-time. I used the money I made to apply to and tour the University of Seattle, Washington. Unfortunately, I was not accepted. I needed new options. Without a college education, I decided to join the Navy. I figured I could serve the country and attend school through the Navy. Joining the Navy was a turning point in my life, but little did I know the challenges that awaited me. As I entered the military world in the 1990's, I learned there was a price to pay for being a Latin woman in a male-dominated environment. Sexual harassment became a harsh reality that I had to face, along with other forms of discrimination, such as being judged for my accent and stereotypes. To add insult to injury, I could not understand relationships with the opposite sex. My first year on active duty was challenging. Overwhelmed by it all, I decided to escape through death and swallowed several pills. My body immediately rejected them, and I vomited all of them up. It woke me up. This experience etched into my spirit and became a foundational source of how I started to support others in the military. I knew that hard work was my greatest strength, and I refused to let anyone define my capabilities. Assigned as a cook, I took it upon myself to prove that I could do that work and more. I worked tirelessly, not only in the kitchen but also in administrative tasks, showcasing my dedication and determination. My efforts did not go unnoticed, and I was given fantastic opportunities in the Navy, including the opportunity to further my education.

Through my studies, I discovered a passion for psychology. I wanted to understand how our experiences shape our reality through our perception of the world and ourselves. I wanted to investigate the human mind. With unwavering determination, I pursued my dream, and in time, I became a psychologist. It was a long and challenging journey, but I knew my experiences had equipped me with a unique perspective and empathy to benefit those in need. My career took an unexpected turn when I was selected to serve at the Naval Inspector General's office. It was a prestigious position. I felt a sense of pride and responsibility as I stepped into this role, knowing I was breaking barriers and paving the way for others like me. I was determined to excel and prove that diversity and inclusion were not just buzzwords but essential components of a successful organization. In that position, I became the advocate for thousands of enlisted Navy Sailors who felt they had no voice!

2017 was one of the most intensive years of my life. I lost my dad while serving as special assistant to the Inspector General. My dad battled Alzheimer's disease in his last years; a cruel condition that slowly stole his memories and recognition of loved ones. I visited him often, and each visit was a heartbreaking experience. He no longer knew who I was, and it was painful to witness his confusion and detachment— although some of these last moments created cherished memories that I still hold onto. One of my favorite memories was his battle against the chickens that invaded his garden. According to my dad, the neighbor had trained the chickens to feast on his precious vegetables. I was home visiting, all dressed up with my hair and makeup done. That day, he designated me the chicken watcher. I spent hours chasing after every chicken, trying to shoo them away from his garden. My dad even tried giving me his cane to nudge them if they weren't moving fast enough. It was a comical sight, but he was not laughing at all. Keeping his garden safe was serious work. Working as the chicken watcher, my day progressed slowly, and exhaustion set in. I had lost a shoe, my hair was frizzy, and I broke a nail. I plopped down next to him on the porch. At that moment, Dad looked at me and asked, "When did you get here?" I exclaimed: "Pappa, I have been here with you all day!" He looked at me incredulously and said, "No, you haven't! I've been here with some stuck-up woman, all day." It was a humorous and unexpected comment, a glimpse of his old self shining through the fog of his illness. At that moment, we laughed together and shared a connection that I will always treasure. That interaction with my dad reminded me never to forget who I truly am. My dad passed shortly after the last time I saw him.

After my dad's death, I immersed myself in my work and was assigned to travel to Japan as a climate assessor. As I assessed the Navy's forward-deployed workplace climates, I heard the voices of the people I spoke with. I shared my findings with my inspection team lead, and he dismissed my subject matter expert opinion regarding the organizational climate and its impact on the mission.

The weight of it all began to take a toll on my health. During this trip, I found myself experiencing intense chest pains, and it was so severe that I had to be rushed to the hospital in an ambulance. The doctors initially suspected a heart attack. It was an anxiety attack, but the experience was a wake-up call for me. I felt that the voices of my fellow sailors were not being heard. I was not afraid to speak up. The issue was that the one person who could have served as a megaphone to address concerns chose to hit the mute button.

A few months later, the organizations I had assessed experienced two catastrophic accidents that resulted in the loss of lives and millions of dollars' worth of damage. I could see the climate that created an environment permissive of shortcuts and exhaustion. I immediately understood that one person can make a difference if those in charge only listen. After the incidents, some high-ranking officers wanted to understand what and why the incidents happened. As a culture and climate assessor, I could not speak of causation but only the correlation between human experience and work performance. I have always been a keen listener. I knew the environment and climate I had assessed two months prior would eventually lead to exhaustion and mistakes that could have catastrophic consequences. When tasked with understanding the culture and its relation to the incidents, I made it my mission to understand the lives of those affected by the accident. I wanted to walk in their shoes to experience their daily routines and challenges firsthand. I knew I had to be their voice because they couldn't speak for themselves. When we presented our findings, some high-ranking officers were furious. They didn't appreciate what we had reported, as it revealed uncomfortable truths. I feared the red flags would get ignored, and something similar could happen again, but I did not hold back. We said what had to be said.

Although the truth is only sometimes well received, the Inspector General ensured our report made its way to the proper authorities, and I discovered that others had also spoken up. Over time, reading through documents, I realized that my work was part of the Comprehensive Review. Many others had echoed equal concerns, and I was relieved to know that I wasn't alone in advocating for attention to the voices of the workforce to drive organizational change.

My experiences in life, as rough and rugged as they were, molded me into the woman I am today, and in this moment, I have a profound appreciation for all of it. They helped me see my experience in the military from a different perspective and taught me invaluable lessons about leadership and the importance of building loyalty. While many people associate the military with harsh and uncompassionate leadership, I quickly realized that recognizing the humanity in others is the key to fostering loyalty and getting the best out of your team. The military is indeed known for its rugged exterior and strict discipline. Many believe you can only be a leader if you curse and scream at people. However, I knew this was a learned behavior and that authentic leadership goes beyond that. It is about recognizing the humanity in people and treating them with compassion and respect. When you care for the person before you, you get a better version of them. Trust, psychological safety, and crucial conversations create awareness, foster loyalty, and generate an environment where everyone's voice is heard. When all voices are listened to, we can achieve remarkable results and create a strong sense of unity within a team. True courage lies in speaking up, raising our voices, and making a difference. When we cultivate this courage within ourselves and others, we have the potential to build individuals and teams capable of achieving anything.

ANGÉLICA KILLION

Emergency Preparedness and Response Coordinator

Angélica Killion is a former small business owner who successfully led a team of Xerox technicians across multiple counties while she held an ASEE degree. In her current role with an electric utility provider, she implements training, operational planning and emergency response, ensuring safer and more efficient outcomes. With a Master's in Supply Chain Management, she is a naturally curious learner and problem-solver who enjoys helping people. Previously, she worked at a shelter for unaccompanied minors. She volunteers as Program Instructor with two Community Emergency Response Teams (CERT) where she educates community members on disaster preparedness and equips them with the skills needed to respond effectively.

From the Known to the Unknown

Vicious cycles in families continue until one person stands up and decides, *no more*. Going against our entire belief system and what family and society want and expect, is hard work. However, these actions are vital for future generations to have a new, healthier norm. It took me decades to become aware of my family's destructive multi-generational patterns. They accepted living a life of conformity—I wanted more. As a first-generation immigrant, taking the familiar path would have been easier, yet true growth comes from paving a new unfamiliar path. I was determined to create a better life and was willing to venture into the unknown to find it. I furthered my education, worked multiple jobs, took many risks, and made the necessary sacrifices to prioritize my future. I faced numerous obstacles along the way, each of which played a role in shaping the person I have become today.

Poverty, alcoholism, violence, and limited education were the foundation that my family was built on for generations. My mom faced a difficult upbringing in Tijuana, Mexico. Living in a humble shack with dirt floors, she and her siblings suffered food insecurity and psychological abuse. Their father often spent his wages at the bar instead of supporting his family. While inebriated, he would aggressively wake up the family in the middle of the night and line them up to yell at them, demanding they answer, "*Aquí quién manda*?!" (Who's the boss here?!). They had to respond that he was over and over again until he was satisfied that his dominance over the household was asserted.

To make matters worse, my mom lost 100% of her hearing in her left ear and most of her hearing in her right ear due to untreated ear infections in her childhood. In addition, she was forced to stop going to school in the sixth grade to help support the family. She loved learning and was devastated.

Despite her harsh upbringing, my mom is a very kind soul. She cared for both of her parents until they passed and has continued to care for other family members throughout her life. When she married, she unintentionally perpetuated the cycle that had afflicted her family by marrying an alcoholic—my father. In the midst of that chaos, she remained resourceful and resilient. My mom was a visionary and with whatever little she had, she created something extraordinary. She used her passport and tourist visa to the U.S. as a tool to design a better future for her children when she insisted that they be born in *el otro lado*, (the other side - as the U.S. is commonly referred to). With this courageous act, she intentionally began the end of the cycle of poverty for our family.

Although my mom crossed the border to give birth, she returned to Tijuana where I lived until the age of eight when my parents divorced and my mom immigrated to the U.S. with me, my brother, and my sister. We faced many challenges including learning the language and culture while trying to navigate the land of opportunity.

We moved in with my aunt and her three children into their two-bedroom apartment in one of San Diego's Barrios for a couple of weeks until things became unbearable. Thankfully, government assistance kicked in and we rented our own apartment in the same complex. Soon after arriving in the U.S., I discovered that some of my family members were selling drugs, buying stolen items, and stealing from their own family. Having come from a disadvantaged country and seeing abundance around me, my young mind could not comprehend their way of life.

My mom was determined to steer us in the right direction regardless of our relatives' destructive actions. My aunt and uncle had an apathetic parenting style, often letting my cousins skip school.

When I asked why they weren't going to school, my mom firmly responded that it didn't matter and that going to school was non-negotiable for us. She knew education was the way to improve our lives and constantly told us, *ponle ganas* (do your very best). She couldn't help with our homework after sixth grade, yet she showed her support by bringing us hot tea and snacks while we worked on our assignments and kept us company late into the night.

From a young age, I have always been inquisitive, constantly questioning the world around me to make sense of it. Growing up between two countries exposed me to different values, behaviors, and beliefs, enabling me to study and appreciate the differences. This opened up my world to greater opportunities and ways of living incorporating both cultures. As a result, I created my own unique path in life.

Nobody in my family had a life I aspired to have. I literally looked across the street to find an example of a more desirable future. My close friend Rachel and both of her parents lived directly across from us in a house with a big backyard. Her grandparents lived around the corner; they were kind and very involved in her life. Rachel's family had two cars and shopped at Price Club (now Costco), bringing home more food and paper towels than I'd ever seen. Having watched my mom stretch our limited groceries to the end of the month and get creative with meals, I wanted more for me and my family.

I overcame numerous challenges growing up including learning the English language and becoming our family's translator and second-in-command in our household from the age of nine. My mom's hearing loss prevented her from learning English. I became the contact person for doctor's appointments, medical insurance, school meetings, and more, often without fully understanding the language and implications to our family. Translating for our family taught me to advocate for myself. Anytime my mom felt disrespected, she insisted on being heard and required me to translate her precise message and sentiment until she felt understood. Starting at the age of ten, I had to look adults in the eyes and tell them that they clearly were unhappy with their current role and should go find another job because my mom insisted I tell them exactly how she felt.

When I was 12, my mom went through the process of obtaining legal permanent status in the U.S.; she wanted to make sure other undocumented Mexican families in the same situation also had access and recruited me to assist. I dedicated countless hours to meticulously completing intricate immigration forms, assisting numerous individuals in their applications for *La Amnistia*, also known as the Immigration Reform and Control Act (IRCA) of 1986. Moreover, I skillfully collected, organized, and generated the necessary supporting documents to substantiate an individual's residency in the U.S. during a specific timeframe. This was a powerful experience—it taught me I can impact lives, regardless of my age.

We relied on government assistance to meet our basic needs of food, shelter, and clothing. My mom became the apartment manager to earn extra income, resulting in more translating for me. I have vivid memories of explaining maintenance issues to the handyman and having him laugh at my limited English vocabulary. This inspired me to master the English language.

With our limited resources, we also took care of my grandfather in Tijuana which meant frequent trips south of the border to buy groceries for both households, as certain items were more affordable there. We often returned home late, even on school nights, and had to spend money on taxis or walk home carrying heavy bags of groceries.

My extended family could be deprecating. At twelve, my aunt predicted I would drop out of school, soon get pregnant, and achieve nothing. I vowed to prove her wrong. Despite ongoing gossip and persistently low expectations, I reached a point where others' opinions no longer mattered. This defensive mechanism allowed me to coexist alongside them while disregarding their behaviors and actions.

The environment I grew up in contradicted everything I wanted for my life. Excessive drinking played a significant role in my extended family gatherings. Unfortunately, this usually led to violence among family members. I witnessed things like a cousin who beat his wife every time he got drunk, an uncle who slammed his head through a police car window as he stood handcuffed outside the patrol car, and adults who neglected their children's needs. Drugs were prominent in our neighborhood. We got to know who was selling and who was buying; we co-existed by keeping our distance. Drug busts were a regular occurrence–as soon as one group of drug dealers was removed, another moved in. Once, as a teenager, a drug dealer from my neighborhood approached my coworker in the car while I was in the passenger seat. I tried to signal him not to approach, yet it was too late–his outstretched hand opened to reveal many colorful balloons containing crack cocaine as my coworker looked in shock. The drug dealer apologized and left, yet that incident marked the end of getting rides from my coworker. These experiences strengthened my passion for change.

At the age of seventeen, I married, unaware that I was continuing a destructive generational pattern within my family. As my relationship descended into a cycle of alcoholism and abuse, I was trapped in a constant state of uncertainty and fear, navigating the challenges of my husband's physical and psychological abuse. His unpredictable behavior haunted me, forcing me to always remain on high alert. I clearly remember how he stood on a freeway bridge, threatening to jump, as I desperately pleaded for him to step back from the edge. This manipulation was one example of the never-ending cycle of chaos that seemed impossible to break free from.

The final encounter with my ex remains etched in my memory. It was at our apartment, a place once filled with hope and dreams which quickly became toxic. I had kicked him out a couple of weeks earlier and he returned to visit our son. During this fateful encounter, I witnessed the true depths of his darkness. He threatened to kill me and our son. He ripped the phone cord out of the wall when I tried calling for help. Thankfully, I was able to call 911 from a second landline and left the receiver off the hook, praying help would arrive in time.

Minutes later, my German Shepherd barked aggressively while officers called out for us to open the door from outside the patio. My ex ignored the officers as long as he could. When he finally opened the door, officers yelled, "We got a call for help. Is everyone okay?" My ex yelled back, "Yes, we are ok" and began closing the door. Seizing my chance, I hurried toward the opening before he could shut it. Swiftly, I yanked the door open, declaring loudly, "No, we're not!" as I pushed my way outside to safety with our baby.

In the midst of the chaos, as we were being interrogated, my ex ran into the apartment, grabbed two large knives, and held them against his chest. He stood defiantly in the doorway of the apartment, facing a sea of police officers with their guns aimed at him. My heart raced as I stood behind the officers, holding our young son tightly in my arms while a helicopter hovered above us. The scene was surreal and served as a chilling reminder of the gravity of the situation.

The standoff continued until my ex dropped the knives and was swiftly apprehended, yet the nightmare was far from over. As he was handcuffed, he searched for me in the midst of the chaos to lock his piercing, rageful eyes on mine and make one final threat—a promise to kill us as soon as he was free.

This harrowing experience was a turning point for me. It was one thing for me to risk my life and quite another to knowingly put my son in harm's way. At this moment, I began my journey down a different, unknown path in search of a new healthier life.

However, I continued to live in fear long after our divorce. My ex stalked me, left random gifts on top of my car, and showed up at my work, school or anywhere he thought I might be.

As time passed, I became aware of the harmful generational patterns of alcoholism and violence affecting my family, extending from my grandmother to my mother and then me. I realized the importance of eradicating these cycles from our future.

Upon deep reflection, I recognized the absence of a consistent positive male influence growing up and wondered how it impacted my life. Visits with our father in Tijuana left a lot to be desired. With my younger siblings in tow, four and eight years younger than me, we set off searching for our father's hangout spot of the day, usually a favorite street corner. Once there, I was responsible for watching my siblings as we stood around being ignored while our father got drunk.

In Mexican culture, family is prioritized above all; however, the cost of staying closely connected to my relatives was too high. When I met my current husband, I was determined to provide a better life for my son and decided to distance us from my extended family, leaving everything we had ever known. I redefined what family meant to me and prioritized life with my son and husband. Taking this unfamiliar path was scary and exciting at the same time.

When my son turned thirteen, we reconnected with my extended family. He questioned why I had kept him away from them, especially his cousins. I explained that I had prioritized his well-being, even if he didn't fully understand at the time. After attending a few family gatherings and witnessing the ongoing drama, he had a better understanding and said, "I now see why you kept me away from all this."

I took the opportunity to return to school after a work-related injury and with my family's support, I finished my Associate's, Bachelor's, and Master of Business Administration while attending school full-time. Halfway through my schooling, our daughter was born, and I chose to stay home to care for her.

How we start matters. Having had few opportunities to participate in activities outside of school due to language barriers, limited finances, and transportation, I searched for extracurricular activities for our children to participate in to engage their body and minds. I wanted to expose them to new experiences while nurturing their interests. Through these activities, they formed new friendships, developed teamwork skills, and gained an appreciation for diverse perspectives, languages, and cultures.

I have always enjoyed helping people and discovered my passion for emergency preparedness and response through volunteering at our local Community Emergency Response Team (CERT). CERT is a group of volunteers trained to be self-sufficient and help others during disasters. Through CERT, I conduct outreach in our community in both English and Spanish and teach people how to prepare themselves and their families for emergencies.

I currently work for an electric utility provider in San Diego, supporting operations and keeping emergency processes updated allowing us to respond safely, quickly, and most efficiently to emergencies and disasters affecting our area. I am grateful to have found a career that brings me joy and allows me to be of service to others.

Through her sacrifices, my mom created numerous opportunities for me and my siblings. Early on, I understood what that meant and vowed to take advantage. She instilled in me a sense of cultural pride and identity and helped me embrace both nationalities – the U.S. and Mexico. She recognized the significance of learning the English language, one of the most widely spoken languages in the world. By always encouraging and supporting me, my mom instilled in me the psychological confidence to advocate for myself and pursue my dreams. Most importantly, in a world full of chaos, my mom created a physically safe space, allowing us to feel protected and secure. I am forever grateful for the opportunities my mom created for me through her selfless sacrifices.

In life, everyone comes to a crossroads where they must choose whether to stay in the warmth of their comfort zone or rip off the layers and venture into the fear and excitement of the unknown. In the unknown lies the possibility of fresh experiences and outcomes. Although it may not be the most straightforward path, it facilitates exponential growth, paving the way for a better life. Fear of the unknown is normal; understanding and transcending it allows us to make progress. With the support of my mom and others, I am blessed to have blazed my own path and found my way to the life I was searching for.

Acknowledgments

I am grateful for the support of many important people in my life who have contributed to my journey. Continuing to shape the life I desire is an ongoing process, and I want to recognize my personal growth and achievements in that pursuit. I am incredibly grateful for my caring and supportive husband, who consistently stands by me through my various endeavors. I appreciate those who made my life difficult, as they inspired me to push harder to reach my goals. To my son José, thank you for your understanding and support as I returned to school. To my daughter Jasmine, your flexibility and openness to learning new things is inspiring and will take you far in life. My in-laws' support in my education and that of our children has been priceless, particularly in nurturing our son's sports interest and our daughters' STEM activities. I appreciate the ESL instructor who taught me English in second grade and the caring teachers who positively influenced my education. Lastly, I want to express my appreciation to Rachel and her family for showing me a better way to live when I needed it most. Overall, I'm incredibly thankful for the support, inspiration, and guidance provided by these significant individuals, as they've played a crucial role in my personal and professional growth.

ALEJANDRA "ALE" SPRAY

Community Empowerment Manager,
Mortenson

Ale manages community participation plans to maximize opportunities for small, women, minority, and other diverse groups on Mortenson's projects. Born and raised in Guadalajara, Jalisco, and a resident of Colorado since 1999, Ale has 20+ years of construction experience. She received her Bachelor of Science degree in Civil Engineering from the Institute of Technology and Higher Studies of the West, in Guadalajara Mexico. Her involvement in the community includes being chairman of the board for the Hispanic Contractors of Colorado, and governor appointed to the advisory council for the Colorado State Minority Business Office. Currently serving on the boards of AdventHealth Avista Hospital, Bellco Credit Union, Mile High Youth Corps, STEMblazers, Colorado Succeeds and the Construction Education Foundation.

The Power of Your Story

After a few months into one of my first leadership programs, I began to deeply reflect on my identity. The more I learned about myself, the more questions arose. Having lived in Colorado for over ten years, I realized that I could no longer simply identify as Mexican, as my home felt different every time, I visited my family. At the same time, I did not consider myself a full U.S.A. citizen yet. This uncertainty about my identity became a source of concern, especially when it came to raising my two kids. I felt lost and unsure of who I truly was.

One Sunday afternoon, a seemingly ordinary trip to the movie theater with my children turned into a profound moment of self-reflection. We were watching the movie "Kung Fu Panda," during a key scene in the film, the main character is confronted by the antagonist who asks, "What are you?" This resonated deeply with me because all my life, especially most recently, I've pondered the same question about my own identity. As I listened to the main character's response, tears suddenly welled up in my eyes, much to the confusion of my children. In that moment, it struck me that I am not simply one thing; I am a complex blend of various roles and attributes. I take pride in being Mexican and an American citizen. I am both a working mom and a professional. I am an engineer, an immigrant, and so much more. Instead of confining myself to a single box or definition, I choose to embrace the multitude of identities that shape who I am. This realization is deeply rooted in the strength and resilience passed down through generations of strong and courageous women in my family. However, this epiphany did not come easily to me, as I often felt burdened by the pressure to conform to society's narrow definition of success.

I was born in Guadalajara, Mexico, to very loving and supportive parents. It was my father who helped guide me towards my passion. He was a civil engineer, often showing me his drawings and explaining his job to me. At one point, I wanted to be an architect, but after learning more about engineering, I became fascinated by the magic of building something tangible from a set of drawings - a home, an office, a bridge, and more structures that are part of a community. I found that my passion was geared more toward how it all came together, and I felt I had the necessary skills, especially in math. One day, I expressed this to my father, acknowledging his energy in the field and expressing my desire to follow in his footsteps in the construction industry as a civil engineer. However, he was hesitant and discouraged me from pursuing engineering, citing the challenges and lack of representation for women in the construction industry, especially in Mexico.

Although his resistance to me entering the construction industry was difficult at first, I believe it was ultimately beneficial that he expressed his concerns and hesitations about my career choice. Those who know me are familiar with the fact that I'm the kind of person who uses others' doubts that I cannot do something to fuel to prove to them and myself that I can do it. That's exactly what I did when he expressed to me his doubts. He became my biggest supporter after I enrolled in civil engineering, and agreed to show me all he knew and help me any way he could. As I was navigating my career, I understood his initial hesitation stemmed from his concern for the challenges, disappointments, and discrimination I might face in the industry as a female, and he didn't want to see his daughter endure those types of challenges.

My parents, coming from humble beginnings, instilled in my brother and me the importance of hard work and earning success. They taught us that wealth wasn't the goal, but rather the power of education and the drive to progress in life. My mother, especially, has been a prime example of what can be achieved with determination. After my parents' divorce when I was twelve, she took on the responsibility of providing for us. Despite my father's presence, he lacked the financial resources to support my mother. Realizing she had to take matters into her own hands, she began saving for a car and college for both my brother and me while we were in middle school.

Upon graduating from high school, we were fortunate enough to receive a new car for college and have our tuition paid to attend a prestigious private college in Mexico. I often tell people that my mother worked hard to provide us with a great education. She held high titles in well-respected organizations despite not having a college education herself, she made it her mission to break the cycle with my brother and me. She emphasized that this was the gift she could give us, and it was now our responsibility to make the most of it.

After a tiring day at work, my mother always made it a priority to come home and genuinely inquire about our day and express concern for our schoolwork, checking our homework and reading bedtime stories. Witnessing her unwavering determination, she became my ultimate source of motivation. Every day, I remind myself that giving up is not an option. My mother never gave up, despite facing countless challenges. With the abundance of opportunities, I have been given, I cannot afford to give up. My mother has made too many sacrifices for me to simply throw it all away, and I could never bear to look her in the eyes and admit defeat just because life gets tough.

I never imagined that my life would take me far from my hometown Guadalajara where I grew up. I went to college planning to continue my life there; little did I know that destiny had other plans in store for me. It all began when I crossed paths with my now ex-husband while he was working in Mexico. He came from the beautiful state of Colorado, and the story goes: boy meets girl, they fall in love and decide to tie the knot which led me to embark on a new chapter of my life where my husband lives in Colorado. However, this decision came with its fair share of challenges. I was the only one in my entire family who had ever ventured beyond the borders of our homeland. My family, consisting of my brother, sister, mother, cousins, and aunts, remained rooted in Mexico. The thought of breaking the news to them about my move to a different state, let alone a different country, was daunting. It was not an easy conversation to have, but I knew that I had to follow my dreams and pursue the opportunities that awaited me. It was a chance for me to grow, learn, and create a better future for myself and for our family. Much to my relief, my family ultimately supported my decision and encouraged me to embrace this new chapter in my life. Their love and support gave me the strength and confidence to face the challenges that lay ahead.

Once the initial excitement of being in a new country wore off, the reality of the situation began to sink in. I found myself in a foreign land, completely unfamiliar with anyone or anything. No family, friends, no access to a car of my own, or a job, except for a small amount of savings that I was trying to be cautious with. Finding employment was a challenge because I didn't have the necessary paperwork, and there was no clear timeline for when I would receive it. There was a level of uncertainty in my life so the decision to wait before starting a family seemed like the right choice at that moment. I needed time to adjust to my new surroundings, to cope with the separation from my family, my culture, my favorite foods, and my friends. I spent six months living in an apartment, and there were moments when I questioned my decision and wondered if it was the right one. Eventually, I came to realize that I had two options: I could either make the best out of the situation or wallow in misery and make everyone around me miserable as well. This was my new reality, my new life, and I had to find a way to embrace it. It was a personal choice to move to another country, not driven by violence or uncertainty in my home country. I had to shift my mindset and figure out how to make the most of my circumstances.

Another shocking aspect of my experience living in this country was the realization that my degree in civil engineering and my professional engineering license from Mexico did not hold the same weight here. I was told that I would need to go back to school and start all over in order to be recognized as an engineer in this country. However, this was not a feasible option for me financially, and I also faced the challenge of not having a strong command of English outside of a classroom setting. This made me feel even more disconnected from my family, my culture, and my roots. It was disheartening to realize that I didn't have the necessary tools to succeed, despite all the hard work I had put into my studies back in Mexico. It felt like all those years I spent earning my degree and completing my dissertation were for nothing. My father's discouragement and belief that engineering was not a suitable career for a woman added to my feelings of uncertainty and lack of direction.

I had limited knowledge of how the education system worked here. I was informed that I needed the transcripts from my college in Mexico, and this was during a time before the Internet, so the process was quite challenging. I got a job at my then-husband's company as a translator. After a year and a half, the company merged with another, resulting in its closure. Suddenly, my ex-husband and I were out of work. While he quickly found a new job, I saw this as a sign to return to the construction industry. I applied to over forty positions, but my lack of a degree and language skills hindered my chances. However, I was determined to seize any opportunity.

Finally, I found a potential opportunity with a company close to where I lived. Taking the advice of showing up at the company and asking for an interview, despite not receiving a call back. Although the interview didn't go well due to my lack of previous experience needed for the role, the owner of the company noticed my determination. When I returned home, I learned that the position I applied for had been filled, but the owner wanted to speak with me about another role.

The owner, a Hispanic man, interviewed me and believed I could contribute to their marketing and estimating team, support. Despite my lack of expertise in that area, he offered me the job. He emphasized that they were willing to teach and support me as long as I put in my best effort. I accepted the job, and it turned out to be a valuable learning experience. The owner, Manuel Gonzalez, became my first mentor in the United States.

I always asked him what drove him to offer me a job. He said that when he saw me filling out the application, he knew that I just needed an opportunity and someone to believe in me. He took a chance on me, and he became my first mentor. Whenever I came up with an idea, he would ask me why I wanted to pursue it and how I planned to make it happen. Sometimes my ideas didn't pan out, but he would always guide and correct me. He was like a mentor and a father figure to me. His belief in me became my motivation. I wanted to prove to myself and to him that I could succeed. Life is full of obstacles, and if I hadn't found that opportunity, things might have turned out differently. But I always try to stay positive and remember that not everything will go my way. What matters is how I react and adapt to the challenges that come my way. I stayed with the company for seventeen years, progressing from estimating to marketing and business development.

As a Latina with an accent, I have faced challenges, biases, and stereotypes throughout my career. My passionate and energetic personality has also been misunderstood and seen as "too much" by some. The lack of representation of Latinas in higher positions within the construction industry is another issue that persists. While there are some Latinas who own their own companies, it is still rare to see young Latin women or men rising into leadership roles in this field. I have personally experienced the struggles of being the only woman in the room and dealing with stereotypes based on my ethnicity and background. Additionally, the language barrier has been interesting to navigate, as engineering in Mexico and the United States have some differences in terms of systems, techniques, and cultural norms. Building a professional network was a challenge for me, as I didn't have any connections or social capital from high school, college, or past jobs to rely on. I had to start from scratch and learn about the business, engineering, and construction politics cultures on my own.

I prioritize my own growth and success over proving myself to others. My children inspire me and give me the motivation to never give up. A mentor of mine, a white woman in construction, once told me, "Nobody gets to tell you where you belong." This phrase has always stuck with me and motivates me to break free from the limitations others try to impose on me. While the industry has made progress in representing women and diverse voices, there is still more work to be done. I will not stay silent and will continue to advocate for diversity, equity, and inclusion in the construction industry.

We need to hold companies accountable for their actions and challenge them to truly embrace diversity, rather than just words. I also ask my colleagues how they are actively working to bring more diversity into our industry. It's not enough to just talk about it; we need to take action and make real changes. It can be exhausting and frustrating at times, but giving up is not an option.

Currently, I am working in a position that focuses on community affairs and outreach. This role has allowed me to use my voice to advocate for the community and support others. It's interesting how my career path has evolved, as I never imagined that I would be working in a position unrelated to my engineering degree, yet

I've learned that success doesn't have a single definition or a linear path. I've come to accept that just because I studied a certain career doesn't mean I have to stay in that field forever. I've taken chances and have said yes to opportunities that have seemed scary and had to be open to unexpected outcomes. Having experienced a time when opportunities were scarce, I now appreciate the real opportunities that come my way. I make them work for me instead of waiting for the "perfect" opportunity. Waiting for perfection can cause you to miss out on valuable lessons and growth. Some opportunities are temporary, some test your humility, and some are short lessons to help you progress. They may be scary and push you out of your comfort zone, but it's important to overcome your fears and seize them because you owe it to yourself. Life is full of challenges and unexpected turns, including divorce, strained relationships, losses, relocations, and opportunities for self-discovery. It is crucial to remember and appreciate what we have achieved, where we come from, and the people who have supported us along the way. For instance, my mother worked tirelessly to ensure I received an education, and a mentor and business owner gave me a chance to prove myself. I feel a deep sense of responsibility to continue fighting, to constantly improve, and to uplift our Latino/ Hispanic culture and heritage. We are not defined by a single narrative. Choosing to cross the border was a decision I made to pursue my dreams, and it does not mean I will settle for less. I take pride in being an ambitious woman, and I firmly believe that it is perfectly acceptable to strive for more for myself, my children, and my community.

While my story may not be unique or extraordinary, I acknowledge that others have faced even greater challenges. Some individuals have had to confront critical issues such as uncertain immigration status or abusive situations. I consider myself privileged because I have never had to worry about being deported, and my American citizenship has made things easier for me.

I believe my story is important and something to be proud of as it is mine, my children know it and recognize it as part of their own heritage too. We all have our own stories, and it's crucial to take ownership of them and be proud of the experiences that have and will continue to shape us. These experiences influence how we engage with our communities, educate others, and interact with our coworkers. Instead of getting angry or feeling entitled, it's important to focus on personal growth and becoming a better person every day. We owe it to ourselves to take care of our own well-being and to be proud of who we are, regardless of our upbringing or the challenges we've faced. These experiences have made us the beautiful individuals we are today. It is part of embracing our culture, our heritage, and our leadership role in this country.

EDUARDO VILLAVICENCIO-VIZCAINO

Speaker | Facilitator | Conversation Curator

Eduardo Villavicencio-Vizcaino is a conversation curator, skilled facilitator, and interactive speaker known for creating engaging and safe learning spaces. With a passion for helping people improve their listening skills, he excels at fostering effective communication throughout organizations.

Eduardo facilitates tailored workshops on a variety of topics including sales, communication, change management, and user experience.

With native command of English and Spanish, and conversational skill in several other languages, he brings a multicultural perspective to his work. Eduardo enjoys traveling and partner dancing, both of which contribute to his mental and physical flexibility.

Libera Tu Legado | Liberate Your Legacy

I am Eduardo Arturo Villavicencio-Vizcaino, a proud U.S.-born son of Ecuadorian immigrant parents. However, it wasn't always easy for me to authentically declare my identity.

Being both first-generation born in the U.S.A. and the first in my family to go to college, presented obstacles to my self-expression and identity.

And in some ways, everyone can be "first generation" in some manner. This could mean being the first in your family to pursue a non-traditional career path, such as becoming a comedian or an artist, instead of a doctor or lawyer.

This can be challenging. I had to navigate the expectations and pressures of my family, who had worked hard and made sacrifices to provide me with opportunities.

My journey to reveal and embrace my life, history, and legacy began later in life when I started to explore my inherited beliefs and expectations.

Be the First, Be Proud

Among the immigrant community, there's a common, sometimes declared, sometimes unspoken, shared value: that being first is important. Being first is the key to a brighter future. In my family, there was an emphasis on education, and being the first to go to college fulfilled one of the dreams my parents had for their children.

Often, being the first at something comes with a sense of accomplishment and celebration. It was the many years of being first in my class and earning 'First Honors' for my grades throughout my school life that made me believe that I would naturally attend the college ranked "first" in the nation!

"¡Sí se puede!"

Although getting into Harvard College from a public school in Los Angeles was a great achievement, my first year there did not feel like anything to celebrate.

I found myself almost 3,000 miles away from home, in a city I did not know beyond the walls of my school, with no laptop, no winter coat, hardly any money, and no network or family. As a seventeen-year-old, I underestimated just how hard it would be since, in the past, my intellect was always enough, but now I was dealing with challenges beyond hard coursework.

There were social and cultural nuances that I was not prepared to face on my own. I had not attended a private school like most of my classmates, and I felt out of place, like I did not belong there.

I recall that my first year was filled with students comparing high school SAT scores and people mispronouncing my last name, often asking whether I was from Mexico. It was often disheartening, and I felt unsupported and isolated.

This resulted in an unexpected "first" for me. I began introducing myself as "Edward" in order to fit in better and avoid detailed explanations of my family background or heritage.

Up until then, I had believed that being the first at something was a good thing. By the end of freshman year, I found myself wishing that maybe I could have just stayed in California.

Little did I know that I would almost lose my choice in the matter of staying in Cambridge, Massachusetts.

Métele/Dale Con Ganas

"Métele o Dale con ganas" is a Spanish phrase that has always resonated with me as a powerful source of motivation and determination. Translated to "Give it your all" or "Put your back into it," it encapsulates the idea of putting your heart and soul into a task, pursuing success with unwavering fervor. While this phrase encouraged me to strive for excellence and persevere through challenges, it has also, at times, unintentionally led me down a path of behaviors I am not proud of.

===

In my freshman year, things took an unexpected turn academically. Despite having fewer classes compared to my senior year of high school, my report card was filled with grades I had never encountered before. I found myself struggling in Japanese class, even failing it, and just barely managing to pass my multivariable calculus course.

Looking back on that period, I've come to realize that I missed out on utilizing the available resources for students in need of assistance. Study halls, office hours, and various forms of academic support were at my disposal, but I believed that I simply needed to work smarter and harder. I can still hear my parents echoing the Spanish expression "Métele ganas" in my mind.

It never occurred to me to reach out and ask for help. I was carrying a hidden sense of embarrassment and shame because I wasn't performing well. By the time I entered my sophomore year, my fixed mindset had me doubting whether I truly belonged there.

As the first semester of my sophomore year progressed, I found myself under immense stress, fearing potential academic probation as I approached my final exams. My sleep was disrupted, and I couldn't concentrate on studying. Instead, I dedicated a significant portion of my time to volunteering in after-school programs within the community and engaging in various forms of community service. Something that provided me with immense joy but also kept my attention away from my studies.

When exam day finally came, I was overcome with nervousness. I contemplated cheating by glancing at my notes when no one was looking. Unfortunately, an exam proctor caught me, and I had to face the consequences.

I vividly remember the moment when I called my parents to share the devastating news. I told my mom about the possibility of being expelled, and she understandably expressed her concern. Then my dad said something that left a lasting impact on me. He said that I didn't necessarily need Harvard or any prestigious institution to be successful and suggested I come back home.

At that moment, standing at a payphone in the middle of Harvard Square, I realized that leaving Boston might mean losing the motivation and confidence to return to complete my undergraduate degree.

As a result of my actions, the college administrative board required me to withdraw as a student. Although I was prohibited from living on campus and enrolling in any classes for one year, it felt like a life sentence. I was embarrassed to break the news to my friends and my community service teammates. people who had expected me to lead a youth program that I founded for the upcoming summer.

It was one of the lowest points in my life.

No Te Rindas

I grew up hearing my immigrant parents often say, "No Te Rindas." This Spanish expression, translating to "Don't Give Up" in English, encapsulates their tenacity, resilience, and unwavering determination in the face of adversity. For many immigrants who leave their homes, families, and every-

thing familiar behind, "No Te Rindas" becomes a touchstone, a source of motivation that reminds them to persevere in pursuit of their dreams, despite the challenges they may encounter along their journey. It serves as a constant reminder to stay strong, push through obstacles, and never lose sight of their goals, ultimately inspiring them to overcome any adversity with unwavering resolve.

===

One thing I knew for certain was that the person I was at home was not who I wanted to be. It was then that I made the difficult decision to stay in the Boston area, even though I only had $400 in my bank account. I was not going to give up, I was determined to find a way to make it work. My father always emphasized the importance of street smarts and being resourceful. He taught me expressions in Spanish like "quítate las anteojeras" which means to take the blinders off and to be alert and aware. I knew he wanted to make sure my brother and I were ready for whatever obstacles we faced. His outlook on life was shaped by his own experiences and the need for practical, survival skills.

Yet, during this period of my life, I was fueled by the echoes of my dad yelling, "Ponte Pilas" – which translates literally to 'put the batteries in.' It's akin to English exhortations like 'get it together' and 'you can do this.' And at this moment, I learned what it meant to really hustle.

At first, I moved off-campus and lived in various local friends' parent's basements or guest houses. I learned to be a valet parker, SAT tutor, bartender, and administrative assistant, and I took the bus everywhere.

In the span of a few months, I slept in seven different homes and had the experience of working five to seven different jobs.

I survived that year. I became resilient. I built grit.

Dios Aprieta, Pero No Ahorca

The Spanish idiom "Dios aprieta, pero no ahorca" carries a profound message about resilience and hope in the face of adversity. Translated as "God squeezes, but doesn't strangle," it emphasizes the idea that life may present us with challenges and difficulties, but these hardships are not meant to overwhelm us completely. Instead, they serve as tests of our strength and character, pushing us to grow and adapt. This idiom encouraged me to persevere through tough times, maintain my faith, and believe that ultimately I will overcome obstacles. It reminds me that even in my darkest moments, there is a glimmer of hope, and with determination and patience, I can navigate through life's trials and emerge stronger on the other side.

===

Throughout my year "off," my mama would check on me often with Sunday morning calls. She knew that was the best time to catch me since I had stopped going to weekly Catholic mass sometime in high school. I could hear the worry in her voice. However, she ended all of the calls with her "bendicion" (blessing) and reminded me to have faith in God's plan.

Eventually, I got an invitation to interview with one of the twenty private schools that I had sent my resume to months earlier. I was surprised since all the other schools had replied that I had lots of experience for someone my age; but they encouraged me to reapply after I had my bachelor's degree and was at least twenty-one years of age.

Fortunately for me, the school director mistakenly read my resume as a graduate of the Harvard Graduate School of Education and asked me to consider serving as head of their Math Department along with teaching a few classes. When I revealed that I was only nineteen years old and still an undergraduate, he apologized for the misunderstanding.

Yet, the hiring committee was impressed by the teaching experience I gained running with the tutoring program that I founded. So, they hired me for a new internship position, secretly folding me in among the twelve teachers who held graduate degrees.

This internship became a huge turning point for me. I discovered a passion for teaching and learning. It restored my self-confidence, provided job stability, and gave me a much-needed sense of belonging. I received praise from my colleagues as a teacher who cared about the students and also supported other teachers by assisting them with basic email and other learning technologies the school was adopting.

Just a few months earlier, I had felt hopeless, ashamed, lost, and alone. But I wasn't alone. My faith in God was renewed as my mom reminded me that "God never gives you more than you can handle."

Life was going so well that I often contemplated forgetting about Harvard and dropping out of college entirely.

No Hay Mal Que Por Bien No Venga

The phrase "no hay mal que por bien no venga" reflects the idea of looking for the positive in a negative situation. It's similar to the English phrase, "every cloud has a silver lining." It describes a situation where something bad has happened, but there may be a positive outcome or opportunity that comes from it if one looks for it.

===

After my required "time away", I found myself back at Harvard, but with a newfound perspective. I approached my second chance at university education with a sense of curiosity and a pair of fresh eyes.

This time around, I had a clear focus on what I wanted to study. Fueled by my experience as a middle school teacher and coach, I eagerly registered for classes that delved into the realms of psychology, sociology, and education, hoping to deepen my knowledge and understanding in these areas.

I found a way to balance my time investment across my studies, my paying jobs, and my local community service. I expanded the tutoring program.

Additionally, I was able to find solace and connection through the Latino/Hispanic affinity groups on campus, providing me with the sense of belonging that I had longed for during my previous stint at Harvard.

As it turns out, the experience of being required to take a year off from studying was a silver lining, because it forced me to get grounded and five semesters later I was ready to become a Harvard graduate.

En Busca De Un Vida Mejor

My immigrant parents constantly reiterated the phrase "Vinimos a este país en busca de una vida mejor" ("We came to this country in search of a better life"). This journey represented a heavy burden, one that could be both a source of motivation and a source of pressure. I understood that my parents had made tremendous sacrifices to provide us with opportunities they never had, and I felt a profound obligation to make the most of those opportunities. It felt that achieving "success" was not just for myself but also for my family and their aspirations.

===

A few days before I graduated from school, I received a call from a prestigious boarding school in the New England area. They offered me a job as a high school math teacher. In addition to teaching math, I also enjoyed coaching volleyball and tennis, being the faculty sponsor for the multicultural student group, and serving as a residential advisor in the boys' dorm.

News spread that my students were engaged by how I used technology to teach math concepts. Within a year, I started conducting workshops for other teachers on how to integrate technology into their teaching methods. The following year, I was recruited by another prestigious school to become their first full-time technology trainer. Over the next few years, I received some mentorship and eventually led the academic and information technology teams. I worked as an IT director for schools, became an IT consultant, and was invited to speak at national conferences about strategies for implementing change in schools.

Despite my professional accomplishments, I felt unsatisfied with my "success" and my choice of career. I could hear my inner critic quietly judging, "Who goes to an Ivy League school to earn a teacher's salary." Unfortunately, my colleagues could also feel my dissatisfaction; I remember one commented that I always seemed like I had "one foot out the door."

It was challenging to find a balance between pursuing my own dreams and goals while also wanting to honor my parents' sacrifices and fulfill their vision of a "better life."

Uno Nunca Sabe

"Uno nunca sabe" is a Spanish phrase that translates to "One never knows" or "You never know" in English. It's used to express uncertainty or the idea that you can never predict with absolute certainty what will happen in the future. It implies that unexpected or unpredictable events can occur, and it's often used when discussing uncertain outcomes or situations where the future is uncertain.

===

The constant feeling that I wasn't living up to my full potential led me to pause my fifteen-year career in K-12 education.

I felt it was time for a change and figured there was something else I was meant to be doing.

As I pondered my next steps, a friend suggested I take the Landmark Forum, a transformative personal development program that he credited as the impetus for starting his own business along with a musical band. At first, I was skeptical. What could a weekend seminar offer that would help me find meaning in my life? However, I decided to give it a try because "uno nunca sabe."

And the course turned out to be a leap into the unknown. During this profound three-day experience, I was invited to objectively look at my past and confront the blind spots and filters that had been affecting my approach to life.

It became clear to me that the assumptions I had about being the son of immigrants informed my expectations about my career happiness, my financial ambitions, and even my prospects for a life companion.

I realized that we grow up hearing jokes, stories, expressions, and other words of wisdom from our parents, their parents, teachers, and religious & community leaders, along with all kinds of media.

Individually, these words and phrases are harmless:

- ❖ Be the First, Be Proud

- ❖ Métele/Dale Con Ganas

- ❖ No Te Rindas

- ❖ Dios Aprieta, Pero No Ahorca

- ❖ No Hay Mal Que Por Bien No Venga

❖ En Busca De Un Vida Mejor

❖ Uno Nunca Sabe

Collectively, over time, my brain accepted and integrated them with our life experiences, adding meaning along the way. These Inherited Conversations can be a burden or a blessing depending on whether we are aware of them and how we have interpreted them, and I was just discovering mine!

Pasos Siguientes | Next Steps

Today I cherish each blind spot I uncover and work to align my authentic dreams and actions. I am proud of my heritage, my name, and the path I've taken. Now I help others discover their blind spots and limiting beliefs. I help them find freedom and power from their inherited conversations as well.

I invite you to explore your own stories and hunt for any ideas that might be limiting your potential in living and contributing authentically to the world.

Ancestral Acknowledgements

Manuel Eduardo Villavicencio Sanchez, Anita Lucia Vizcaino Sotomayor, Marcos Constantino Wilson, Richard E. Barbieri

- 292 -

CONSEJOS

ROCÍO PÉREZ

- ❖ **Do what makes your heart sing:** Prioritize activities that bring joy, happiness, and fulfillment to your life.

- ❖ **Do the inner work:** Confront your fears and actively work towards overcoming the experiences that hinder your progress.

- ❖ **Continually self-reflect:** Self-awareness allows you to make positive changes and live life on your terms.

ADRIANNA ABARCA

- ❖ Surround yourself with talented people who share your convictions and goals.

- ❖ Have a vision of your future and go after it. You may not have what you need right now, but you can do almost anything if you believe in yourself, are passionate, and work hard.

- ❖ Above all, know yourself and never give up.

JOSÉ BETETA

- ❖ **You either sink or swim:** I sulked for two months following my graduation, having some of the best grades in my school and several College offers, but no legal status to exercise. My stepfather, whom I loved very much, was an amazing father figure, and the greatest role model on how to be a devout father, was an amazing support to me since I was five years old, told me that if I decided to stay any longer where I resented my place in the world, that I could do so and sink, or I could apply myself, use my intelligence and swim. I chose the latter and never looked back. Not merely words, but a change in attitude that led to me opening so many doors for me and others. Thanks Dad, R.I.P.

❖ **Things are not over when you think they're over:** When a financial institution tells you that things cannot be done, this does not mean this is the end of things. Many new businesses waste time and efforts restarting their application process, which could easily take two to three months, had they only asked the bank what to do from that point forward. There's lots you can do.

❖ **You are your biggest obstacle:** As soon as I began to rid myself from limitations like family norms, community and social impositions, religious and other beliefs that didn't fit my heart, personality and humane disposition, single tracked schools of thought, parental norms that were the norms and in some cases unquestionable laws, and my close circle biases, I became free to think beyond the unimaginable like never before. I was able to explore outside of things that tied me down mentally. From that point on It was easy to then understand the concept of endless possibilities.

TAMIL MALDONADO VEGA

❖ Build / Prepare yourself to be able to help build others.

❖ There is power in collaboration, participation and community engagement.

❖ Cultural heritage has value and can become a powerful asset.

JERRY NATIVIDAD

❖ Believe in yourself regardless of your race, cultural, ethnic, status, or gender. These things do not define you or hinder your abilities.

❖ Harness the energy and greatness that God has bestowed upon you. You have the same potential as anyone else.

❖ Be proud of being American and being a Latino man or woman. Don't let anything hinder your progress because of your ethnicity or gender.

GIL JUAREZ

❖ Try, fail, learn, try again.

❖ Leaders get paid for the tough times; appreciate the hard as much as the good, the hard is where growth and the opportunity to be your best lies.

❖ You are often your own biggest obstacle, trust yourself, forgive yourself, and love yourself.

MARTHA NIÑO RODRIGUEZ

❖ Ask and Give specifics. We don't know what we don't know. Being specific about what we want and specific of the advice we give is KEY.

❖ Being the first is hard and chances are you might be the only one that looks like us doing it, congratulations YOU ARE A CYCLE BREAKER. Focus on that.

❖ The best network contacts are your friends. Get to know people one layer deeper and focus on building friendships – the network part is just a bonus.

SILVIA ELIAT

- ❖ Don't stop believing.

- ❖ Move forward – always.

- ❖ Live, love, learn, laugh.

CARLOS QUEZADA

- ❖ **The transformative power of personal growth:** Personal growth can have a profound impact on our lives. However, to do so we must embrace change and challenges as opportunities for growth and self-discovery.

- ❖ **Overcoming obstacles leads to success:** Overcoming Obstacles is Key to Success: Facing and conquering challenges can lead to personal fulfillment and the attainment of goals.

- ❖ **The importance of helping others:** By building strong partnerships and taking bold actions, we can make a positive impact on the lives of others and experience a sense of fulfillment in the process.

MARK MADRID

- ❖ There is a redeeming power in forgiveness.

- ❖ A whole lot of little goes a long way (don't underestimate the smallest of progress)!

- ❖ Have integrity and make the right call, even when doing so is uncomfortable.

STACI LATOISON

❖ Learn about money, invest in yourself, be intentional about money and time, continue to stay a student of life, and do things differently than those around you.

❖ Listen to your own advice. Don't just encourage others to go for their dreams. Invest in yourself and chase your dreams.

❖ Too often we think too small and only for today. This limits our potential. Invest in your highest yielding asset- You.

GERARDO GARCIA-JURADO

❖ **Embrace diversity:** Understand and appreciate the rich tapestry of cultures within the Hispanic community and the broader American society. Embracing diversity enhances personal growth and enriches the collective experience.

❖ **Persistence pays off:** Be prepared for challenges, especially as an immigrant. Legal and employment hurdles may seem daunting, but persistence and determination can lead to opportunities and success.

❖ **Give Back to the community:** As you progress in your journey, remember to support and empower others in your community. Collaborate with organizations and initiatives that promote education, diversity, and community development. Your contributions can make a meaningful impact.

PEDRO DAVID ESPINOZA

❖ Discipline and focus make you successful.

❖ It's important to ask yourself, what negative trends and habits do you have. Then answer honestly and work towards correcting them.

❖ Preparation is the X factor.

MARCIA V. MORENO

❖ Create your own definition of success, and don't let others define what that means to you. The definition changes and evolves over time; Success looks like you.

❖ Embrace your accent, don't try to "reduce" it. It is who you are, it shows your courage to get out of your comfort zone, your growth mindset and your global upbringing. Be proud!

❖ Pay it forward: I am here because of so many Latinos who extended their arms to welcome me. I am here because I had a village who supported me, embraced me and offered their backs when I needed it. I will do the same for as long as I can.

SAUL GOMEZ

❖ Find a group of people who challenge and inspire you, spend a lot of time with them, and it will change your life forever.

❖ Your truth is your truth, but it doesn't make it THE truth.

❖ You can't fill someone else's cup from an empty one – make sure you fill your own cup too.

JOANNE SIRACUSA

❖ Investing in yourself is the most valuable investment you can make.

❖ Learn to recognize what is truly important and what isn't.

❖ Spread kindness and generosity to those around you. Whether it's volunteering, paying for someone's meal, or simply offering a kind word or a listening ear to a friend in need, every act of kindness can make a real difference.

PAM COVARRUBIAS

❖ **Embrace inner healing:** Take time to connect with your inner child, understanding the healing power that comes from acknowledging and addressing past wounds.

❖ **Navigate challenges with resilience:** Learn from personal challenges and adopt a resilient mindset, recognizing that life's difficulties can be transformative opportunities for growth.

❖ **Explore self-identity:** Engage in a journey of self-exploration to understand your identity, especially in the face of societal expectations, and embrace the uniqueness that makes you who you are.

MAVI BARRAZA

❖ Visualize, see your future before it comes true.

❖ Persist, regardless of the challenges; keep moving forward.

❖ You got this!

VERONICA LAWRENCE ORTEGA

❖ You must work on yourself, before you can truly help others.

❖ If you are drowning try to stand up, sometimes the water is not really that deep.

❖ Training yourself: You did not lose, you gained experience.

ANGÉLICA KILLION

I discovered the poem below as a pre-teen; it served as my inspiration for persevering when things got tough and to this day, it remains on my desk as a reminder to keep moving forward.

Don't Quit

When things go wrong, as they sometimes will,

When the road you're trudging seems all uphill,

When the funds are low and the debts are high,

And you want to smile, but you have to sigh,

When care is pressing you down a bit,

Rest, if you must, but don't you quit.

Life is queer with its twists and turns,

As every one of us sometimes learns,

And many a failure turns about,

When he might have won had he stuck it out;

Don't give up though the pace seems slow—

You may succeed with another blow.

Success is failure turned inside out—

The silver tint of the clouds of doubt,

And you never can tell how close you are,

It may be near when it seems so far,

So stick to the fight when you're hardest hit,

It's when things seem worst that you must not quit.

– Unknown

ALEJANDRA "ALE" SPRAY

❖ Never forget to pay it forward. No one made it completely alone, we are a community and we lift each other as such.

❖ Getting out of your comfort zone is daunting though is when the growth takes place.

❖ Be proud of your heritage, your story, your culture. All of them combined are the compass to use along your journey.

EDUARDO VILLAVICENCIO-VIZCAINO

❖ The most powerful three letter word is YET. I tell my clients and audience members to add that to the end of their "I Don't Know" and "I Can't" phrases.

❖ Turn your inner critic into an inner coach by referring to yourself in third person. **Distanced self-talk** helps us relate to ourselves like we were someone else, putting us in a position to think more objectively about our circumstances and work through them effectively.

❖ Learn to use Artificial Intelligence (A.I.) tools to time travel to the **FUTURE you**. During challenging times, ask *that* version of you what you want the CURRENT you to know.

QUOTES & PHRASES
THAT WE LIVE BY

ROCÍO PÉREZ

❖ *"Every man must decide whether he goes for it or whether he contemplates the successes of another." – Unknown*

❖ *"Thought is the original source of all wealth, all success, all material gain, all great discoveries and inventions, and of all achievement." – Claude Bristol*

❖ *"Imagination is more important than knowledge. For knowledge is limited, whereas imagination embraces the entire world." – Albert Einstein*

❖ *"Your mind is a powerful thing. When you fill it with positive thoughts, your life will start to change." – Unknown*

❖ *"I learned that courage was not the absence of fear, but the triumph over it. The brave man is not he who does not feel afraid, but he who conquers that fear." – Nelson Mandela*

ADRIANNA ABARCA

❖ *"We must educate our children through personal examples and strong belief that ongoing learning is essential."*

❖ *"Latinidad is a feeling of unity among Latinos."*

❖ *"It is essential to help our children understand the world we live in."*

❖ *"We must have the most accurate representation possible to improve this world. It is on each of us to work to ensure our stories are told accurately and completely."*

❖ *"Acknowledging the country of origin of our fathers does not take away from our love of the U.S. It enhances our connection to all of America."*

JOSÉ BETETA

❖ "Learn from *a river; obstacles may force it to change its course, but never its destination." – Matshona Dhliwayo*

❖ *"No act of kindness, no matter how small, is ever wasted." – Aesop*

❖ *"Integrity is doing the right thing, even when no one is watching."* – *C.S. Lewis*

❖ *"There is no failure except in no longer trying."* – *E. Hubbard*

❖ *"Love does not consist in looking at each other, but in looking together in the same direction."* This last quote was by Antoine de Saint-Exupéry, author of *The Little Prince*, a very special book in our family. I am still learning how to live by this quote, looking in the same direction as my wife, trust me, I try very hard, but she makes it very difficult for me because she is very hard not to look at.

TAMIL MALDONADO VEGA

❖ *"There's hope every time we work for something."* – *Tamil Maldonado Vega*

❖ *Ode to the hands that work. "Alabanza Oda a las manos que trabajan." – Juan Antonio Corretjer (Adapted from Oubao Moin)*

❖ *"Individuality within the collective goals makes the dream work. Everyone can participate in creating change by utilizing what you have now to give back to the community and help, however small or big, that may be, everything adds to accomplish the vision."* – *Tamil Maldonado Vega*

❖ *"Individually, we may not be perfect due to our human nature, but together we have the potential to achieve perfection by compensating for each other's weaknesses and thriving as a collective."* – *Tamil Maldonado Vega*

❖ *"Research and knowledge research is crucial because it can not only open doors for individuals and their children but also for their community." – Dra. Luz Amelia Vega Rodríguez (My Mother)*

GIL JUAREZ

❖ *"I have met the enemy, and he is I." – G. Juarez*

❖ *"Demand not that events should happen as you wish; but wish them to happen as they do happen, and you will go on well." – Epictetus, Discourses*

❖ *"The child who is not embraced by the village will burn it down to feel its warmth." – African proverb*

❖ *"If you quit today, you'll quit every other hard day of your life." – Coach Ian Cummings*

❖ *"Fear is the mind killer." – Frank Herbert, Dune*

MARTHA NIÑO RODRIGUEZ

❖ *"Looking for diversity – look in diverse places."*

❖ *"Better is different for everyone."*

❖ *"We all have Imposter Syndrome in one way or another – the difference is who fights for it the hardest."*

❖ *"Hope, Help, Hustle – Hope = belief, Help = others, Hustle = work."*

❖ *"Being poor in the U.S.A. is so different than being poor in a third world country."*

SILVIA ELIAT

❖ *"Great things happen to those who don't stop believing, trying, learning and being grateful." – Roy T. Bennett*

❖ *"It's your reaction to adversity, not adversity itself that determines how your life's story will develop." – Dieter F. Uchtdorf*

❖ *"Not in doing what you like, but in liking what you do is the secret of happiness." – J.M. Barrie*

❖ *"The art of life is to know how to enjoy a little and to endure very much." – William Hazlitt*

❖ *"The two most important days in your life are the day you are born and the day you find out why." – Mark Twain*

CARLOS QUEZADA

❖ *"As Latino immigrants, we carry the flame of hope that lights the way for a brighter future." – Carlos Quezada*

❖ *"We are not just dreamers; we are the architects of our destinies. As Latino immigrants, we build bridges to new horizons, creating a legacy of determination and success." – Carlos Quezada*

❖ *"El camino hacia el éxito es como una escalera única para cada uno, donde cada escalón cuenta la historia única de nuestras experiencias y esfuerzos." – Carlos Quezada*

❖ *"Success begins with curiosity; ask questions, seek knowledge, and embrace the unknown." – Carlos Quezada*

❖ *"The triumphant journey to success is paved with curiosity, courage, and authenticity; dare to explore, strive to be bold, and stay true to who you are." – Carlos Quezada*

MARK MADRID

❖ *"Live a great story, even when times are tough."*

❖ *"Faith is the substance of things hoped for, the evidence of things not seen." – Hebrews 11:1*

❖ *"We are what we repeatedly do. Excellence, then, is not an act but a habit." – Aristotle*

❖ *"Sigue adelante (Keep going)!"*

❖ *"It's nice to be important, but it's more important to be nice (thank you, Nina Vaca!)."*

STACI LATOISON

❖ *"The future of leadership is female. Organizations and businesses thrive with women at the helm. Think about what could be accomplished if 50% (or more) of CEO's were women."*

❖ *"Tap into your greatness. Understand what you have to offer with confidence. That is your "unique value proposition."*

❖ *"Stand confidently in your power and challenge yourself to dream bigger."*

❖ *"Dream big, advocate for and invest in yourself, and don't let fear hold you back."*

❖ *"We don't grow up talking about money in our households, but financial literacy is essential as we are faced with financial decisions each and every day of our lives."*

GERARDO GARCIA-JURADO

❖ *"You'll never make it in a mainstream advertising agency here in the States." – Andrea M.*

❖ *"My heart raced at the prospect of conquering the Big Apple."*
– Gerardo Garcia-Jurado

❖ *"I've encountered many similar anecdotes over the years, reminding me of my impact on inspiring others despite my unique circumstances."*
– Gerardo Garcia-Jurado

❖ *"It's humbling to acknowledge that they often have a deeper under-standing of Latin American culture than I do myself."*
– Gerardo Garcia-Jurado

❖ *"Our core values—family, hard work, optimism, and warmth—have played an integral role in shaping this great nation."*
– Gerardo Garcia-Jurado

PEDRO DAVID ESPINOZA

❖ *"You don't have to be a millionaire to help a millionaire." – Susan Hyatt.* This advice is key, you don't have to be CEO to help CEOs. We all need each other. When I work with people I put the human hat first, I'm relational over transactional, I seek commonalities, and I am intentional in finding our common vision.

❖ *"You don't need a title to be a leader." – Mark Sanborn*

❖ *"It's people that lead businesses. Businesses do not lead businesses."*
– Eric Schmidt, Trillion Dollar Coach; The Leadership Playbook of Silicon Valley's Bill Campbell.

❖ *"People are the most important asset of a company. CEOs are chief emotional officers. Empathy is key. Remember, that you don't need anyone to promote you to be you and that you are the architect of your own career." – Chip Conley*

❖ *"I see how broken the world is and how God is using me to love them. Not by preaching, but by getting to know them, praying for them, and just loving them."*

MARCIA V. MORENO

❖ *"Caminante no hay camino, se hace camino al andar."*
– Antonio Machado, (English: Wayfarer, there is no way. Make your way by going farther.

❖ *"Many small people, in small places, doing small things can change the world." — Eduardo Galeano*

❖ *"Wherever you go, go with all your heart." — Confucius*

❖ *"Numb the dark and you numb the light." — Brene Brown*

❖ *"Courage starts with showing up and letting ourselves be seen." — Brene Brown*

SAUL GOMEZ

❖ *"The devil saw me with my head down, and thought he won — until I said, 'AMEN.'"*

❖ *"I prefer walking alone in truth, than to walk with many in deceit."*

❖ *"I'm humble because there can always be less; I'm grateful because I've had less." — Anonymous*

❖ *"The discomfort you are avoiding is keeping you from the success you seek."*

❖ *"Lead me, follow me, or get out of my way." — Thomas Paine*

JOANNE SIRACUSA

❖ *"There is power in perseverance, purpose in pain, growth in the process, and beauty in the journey." — Joanne Siracusa*

❖ *"We radiate positive energy when we undergo personal growth and transformation, which brings profound changes in our environment." — Joanne Siracusa*

❖ *"Take time to appreciate your strengths and forgive yourself for your faults. Practice self-care and make time for things that bring you joy." — Joanne Siracusa*

❖ *"Let's break the cycle and spread the love we never received." — Joanne Siracusa*

❖ *"It's about embracing my own path and making decisions that align with my values." – Joanne Siracusa*

PAM COVARRUBIAS

❖ *"Life unfolded, and I had no choice but to turn to the little girl for answers. She taught me how to set down my anger and resentment, how to live free of all the burdens of the past."*

❖ *"My mother's guidance taught me the importance of considering my options and making thoughtful choices before taking any action. The power of choice became part of my foundation as an adult."*

❖ *"The story of my life has been written with the pen of my choices, embracing the power of choice at every turn."*

❖ *"Through the power of storytelling, I have found healing and growth, expanding the possibilities that lie before me."*

❖ *"My life changed when I asked myself, 'What can I do to make money with skills that I have and that I don't have to learn?'"*

MAVI BARRAZA

❖ "The difference between a successful person and others is not a lack of strength, not a lack of knowledge, but rather a lack in will." – Vince Lombardi

❖ *"El perdón es una decisión, no un sentimiento, porque cuando perdonamos no sentimos más la ofensa, no sentimos más rencor. Perdona, que perdonando tendrás en paz tu alma y la tendrá el que te ofendió."* (Forgiveness is a choice, not a feeling, because when we forgive, we no longer feel the offense, no longer harbor resentment. Forgive, for in forgiving, you will have peace in your soul, and so will the one who offended you.) *– Madre Teresa de Calcuta*

❖ *"The future belongs to those who believe in the beauty of their dreams." – Eleanor Roosevelt*

❖ *"I was born with something inside of me that refuses to settle for average. I'm not quite sure what it is, but I'm grateful to have it." – Unknown.*

❖ *"Believe you can and you're halfway there." – Theodore Roosevelt*

VERONICA LAWRENCE ORTEGA

❖ *"The happiness of your mind depends on the quality of your thoughts." – Marcus Aurelius*

❖ *"I am not who who you think I am; I am not who I think I am, I am who I think you think I am." – Charles Horton Cooley*

❖ *"If you do not like where you are, move you are not a tree." – Hetal Chirag*

❖ *"Find out who you are and do it on purpose." – Dolly Parton*

❖ *"The quickest way to find out who you are is to discover who you are not." – Mathew McConaughey*

ANGÉLICA KILLION

❖ *"We are what we pretend to be, so we must be careful about what we pretend to be." – Kurt Vonnegut, Mother Night.*

❖ *"Success is not final, failure is not fatal: It is the courage to continue that counts." – Winston Churchill*

❖ *"Do not go where the path may lead, go instead where there is no path and leave a trail." – Ralph Waldo Emerson*

❖ *"Focus on the ultimate goal, because more than one thing will get you there."*

❖ *"Challenge expectations, don't conform."*

ALEJANDRA "ALE" SPRAY

- ❖ *"When so much is given, so much is expected." – Luke 12:48*

- ❖ *"Unless you ask, you will never know the answer."*

- ❖ *"Believe in yourself and never doubt the spot you have earned."*

- ❖ *"No one gets to tell you where you belong."*

- ❖ *"Throw dirt at me and watch me blossom." – Frida Kahlo*

EDUARDO VILLAVICENCIO-VIZCAINO

- ❖ *"The best relationships or results in my life were found on the other side of a conversation I was hesitant to START. Now, I use FEAR as a compass for my HEART !!"*

- ❖ *"Don't believe everything you think." – Joseph Nguyen*

- ❖ *"The phrase 'I know that' is an instant learning killer.'"*

- ❖ *"When I hear myself or someone else say the phrase 'on the other hand', I stop and ask, 'What's the third option I'm not seeing?'"*

- ❖ *"Just because I speak with an accent doesn't mean that I think with an accent..." – Alberto Aragon*

EPILOGUE

To all the readers who embark on this life-changing journey with us,

We extend our deepest gratitude for choosing to dive into the pages of *Fortaleza*. This book is a testament to the indomitable strength of the human spirit and the boundless potential that resides within each and every one of us.

Within these stories, you will find inspiration, motivation, and encouragement to rise above life's challenges. As you immerse yourself in the experiences shared by the twenty-two co-authors, you will discover a profound sense of connectedness. You will realize that you are not alone in your struggles, and that within you lies the power to transform your life.

Fortaleza is the armor we all need to face adversity head-on. It is the unwavering strength that refuses to yield, even in the face of the most daunting obstacles. It is the force that can turn the tide of any situation in our favor. Through these pages, you will learn to see beyond your challenges and draw strength from them. You will uncover a world never before experienced—a world where you are different, and where your dreams can become a reality.

Shift the narrative of "what's happening *to* me" to "what's happening *for* me." Discover the magic that lies within the work you often avoid. Realize that you already possess everything you need to succeed—your wisdom, your energy, and your essence. *Fortaleza* will guide you in harnessing these inner resources and channeling them towards creating a happy, healthy, and meaningful life.

The twenty-two co-authors in this book have bared their souls, sharing their own struggles and triumphs in the hopes of inspiring and educating others. They have faced complex challenges and have emerged stronger, wiser, and more resilient. By sharing their stories, they aim to help you avoid making the same mistakes and to provide the inspiration you may need as you navigate your own journey.

As you close this book, remember that *Fortaleza* is not just a concept or an idea—it is the internal strength that will guide you through life's storms with grace and determination. Embrace it wholeheartedly, and you will discover that every challenge is an opportunity in disguise.

May the wisdom and experiences shared within these pages fuel your dreams, propel you forward, and transform obstacles into stepping stones. May you find the strength to push through, learn, and grow. And may you realize that within you lies the power to create the life you've always dreamed of.

Con Gratitud,

Co-Authors, *Fortaleza*

ACKNOWLEDGEMENTS

We are forever grateful to each and every one of our co-authors: Adrianna Abarca, Alejandra "Ale" Spray, Angélica Killion, Carlos Quezada, Eduardo Villavicencio-Vizcaino, Gerardo Garcia-Jurado, Gil Juarez, Jerry Natividad, Joanna Siracusa, José Beteta, Marcia Moreno, Mark Madrid, Martha Niño Rodriguez, Mavi Barraza, Pam Covarrubia, Pedro David Espinoza, Saul Gomez, Silvia Eliat, Staci LaToison, Tamil Maldonado Vega, and Veronica Lawrence Ortega for your unwavering dedication, love, compassion, and empathy throughout your challenging journey. Despite the numerous trials and tribulations you faced, you kept moving forward, inspiring us all and showing us what is possible. Your stories are a testament to the power of resilience of the human spirit and will undoubtedly motivate and inspire readers to see beyond their own challenges, find strength through adversity, and explore new and different worlds. Thank you for pouring your hearts into bringing this book to life. *May the ripples of your impact echo through eternity.*

A huge thank you goes to Gerardo Garcia-Jurado, for his exceptional work in designing the *Fortaleza* book cover, webpage, and marketing materials. His expertise in global marketing and branding has been invaluable in bringing this life-changing work to life. I am truly grateful for his countless hours and unwavering dedication in making this work of art a reality.

Thank you to our editors, Roy Love and Shareen Rivera, for capturing our voices, intention and impact, and for your editing talent.

A heartfelt thank you goes to our book consultant, Shareen Rivera, for her invaluable guidance throughout the entire book journey. Your exceptional talents and skills are evident on every page of our book. We are immensely grateful for the countless hours you dedicated to supporting us in bringing this book to life. Your unmatched work ethic, including working late into the night, waking up early, and staying up all night to ensure that every aspect of the book flourished. Once again, thank you for your unwavering dedication and commitment.

Fortaleza co-authors expresses sincere gratitude to Adrian Mendoza of Mendoza Ventures for his contributions to our book. Adrian's support in setting the foundation, guidance in the book writing process, and firsthand experience in publishing his own books has been invaluable.

To our family, loved ones, and friends, thank you for your love, all that you did, and sacrifice to ensure we shared our stories with the world. Thank you, Thank you, Thank you.

To our readers, thank you for believing in your dreams and bringing them to fruition. May everything you touch turn into gold.